Adult Coloring Book:
Butterfly Designs and Patterns
for Stress Relief and Relaxation

First Printing, 2016

ISBN 978-0-692-67239-6

Included in this book are 32 butterfly designs to help you relax and explore your creativity. Remember there is no right or wrong way to color. Instead, take a nonjudgmental approach and immerse yourself in the simple act of artistic expression. Happy coloring!

*Colored pencils are recommended as other coloring media may bleed. We've included a test page if you would like to test other media.

test page

table of contents

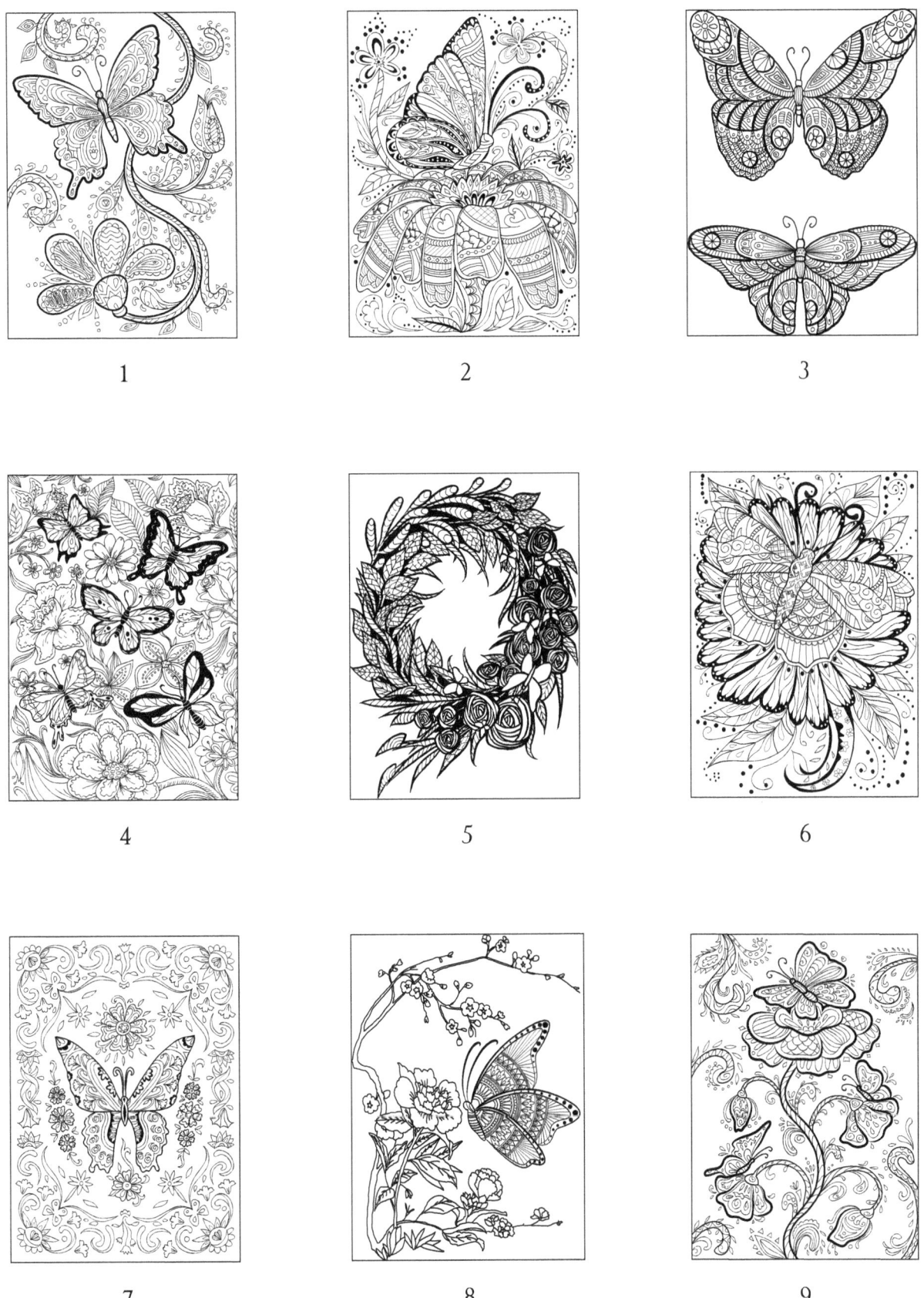

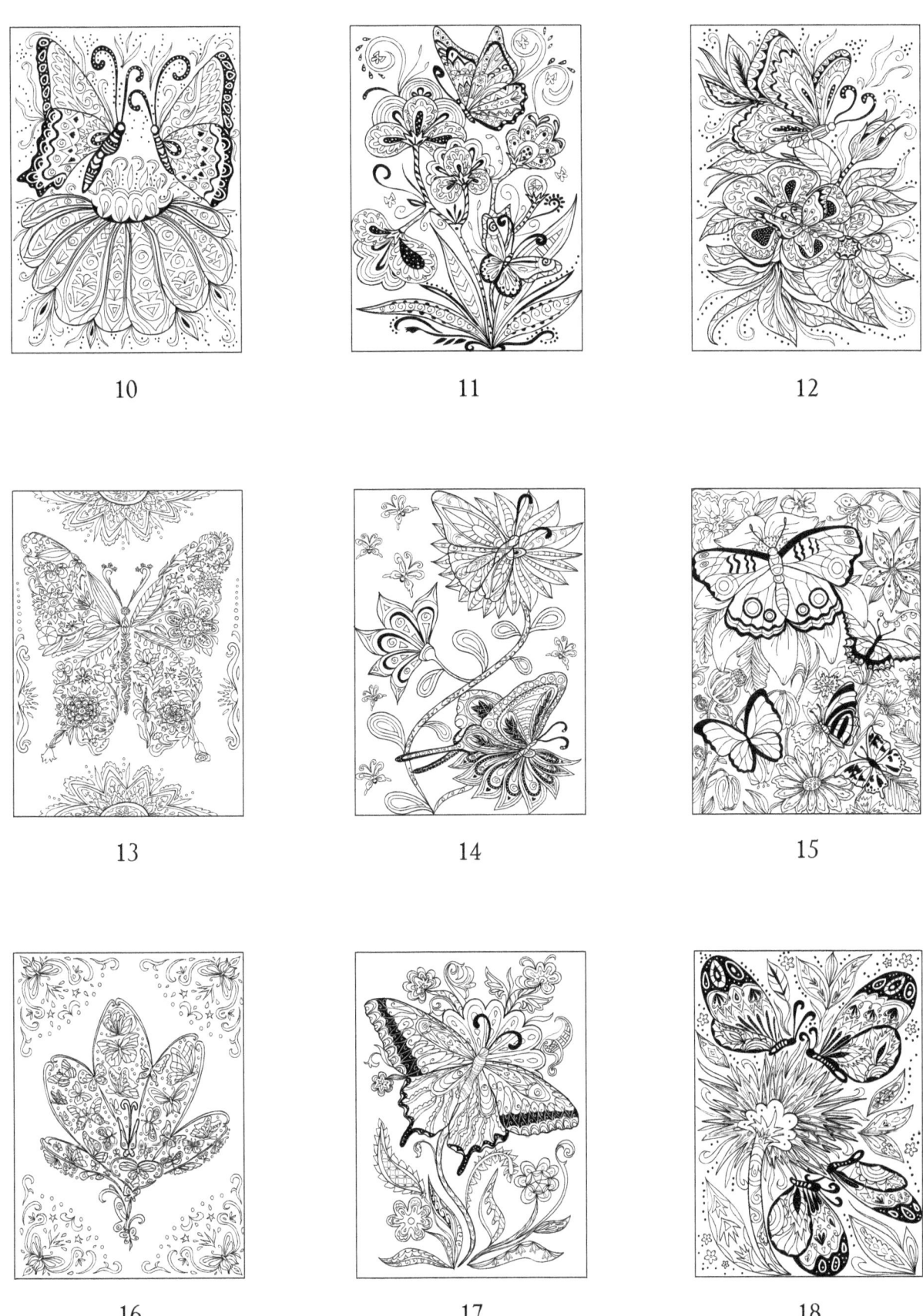

10

11

12

13

14

15

16

17

18

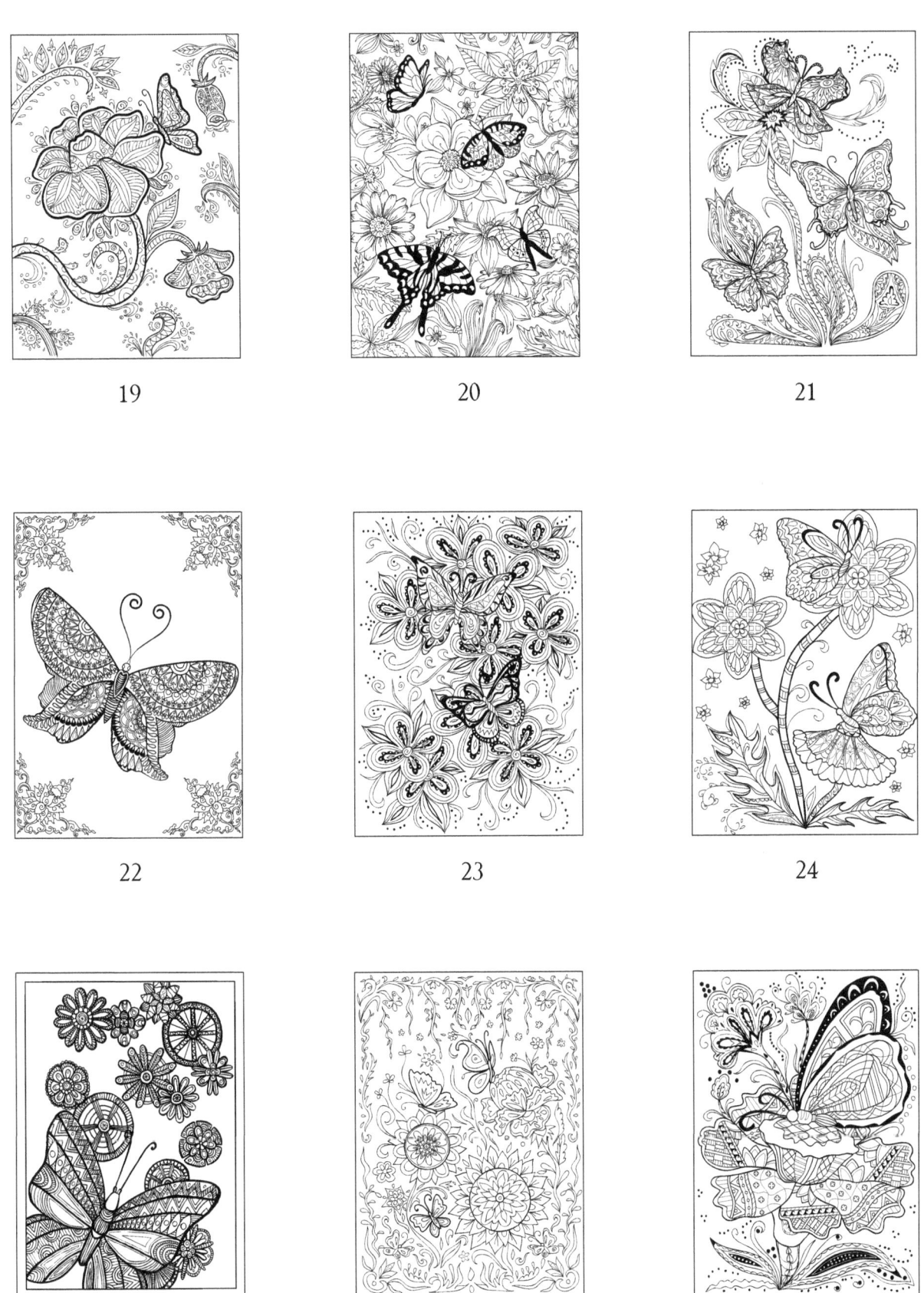

19

20

21

22

23

24

25

26

27

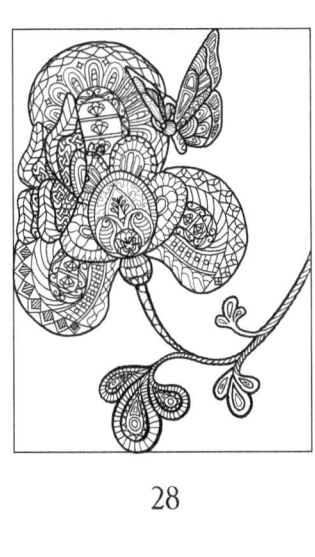

28

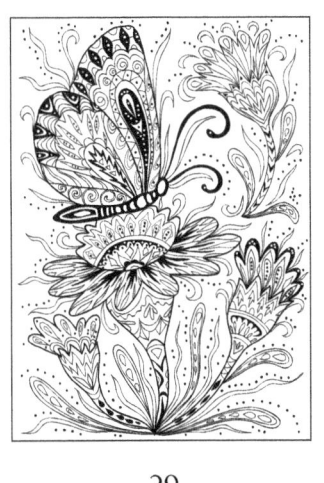

29

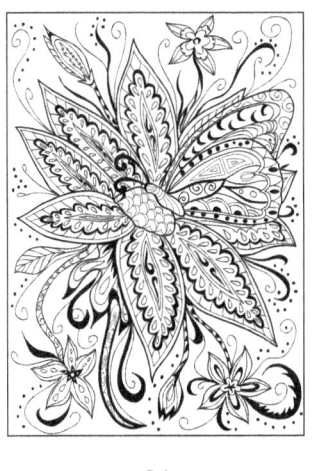

30

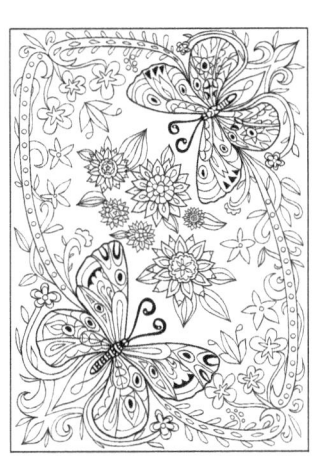

31

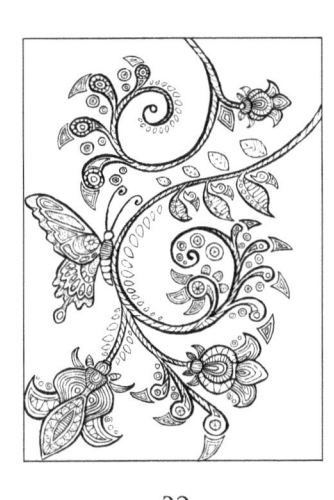

32

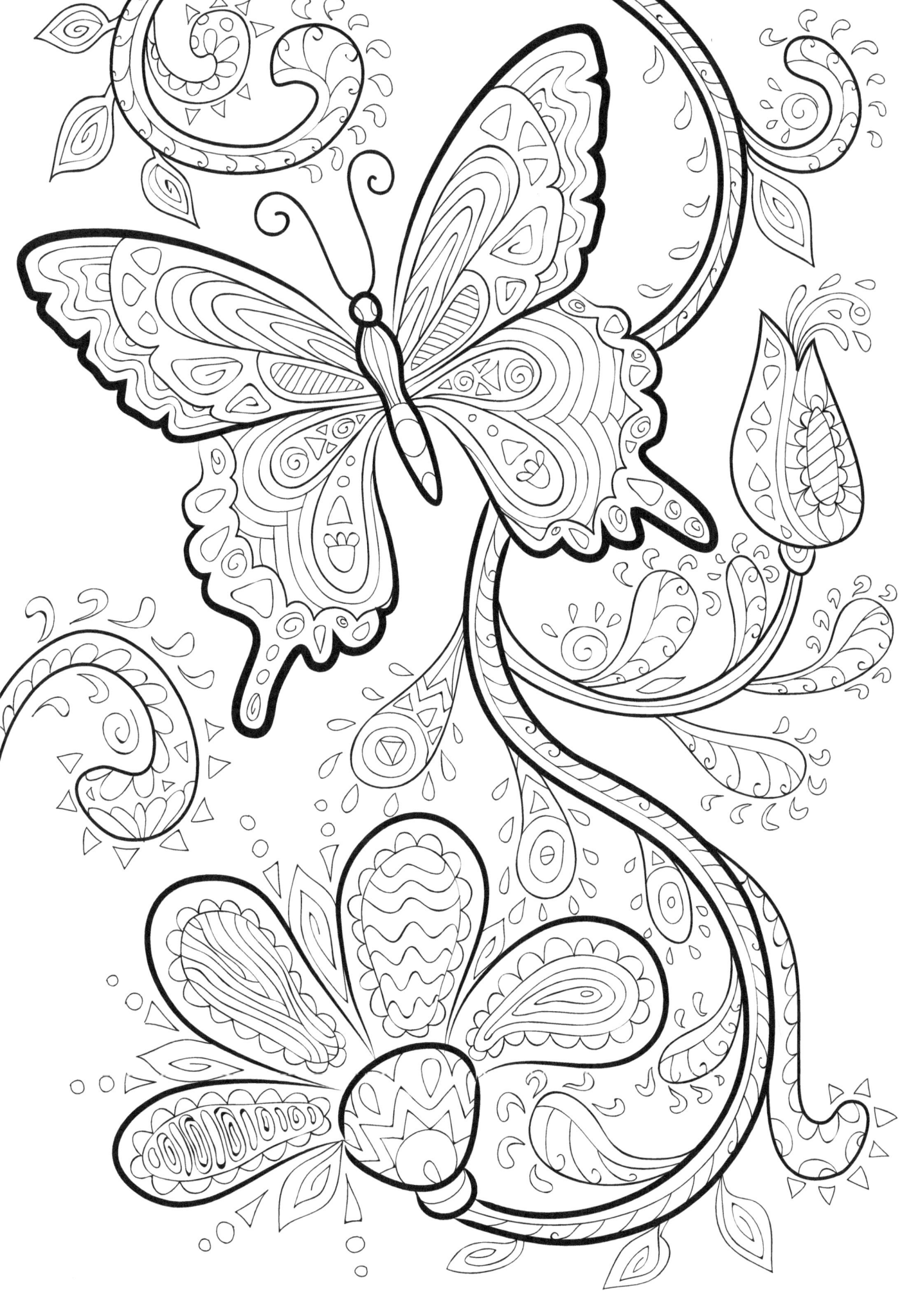

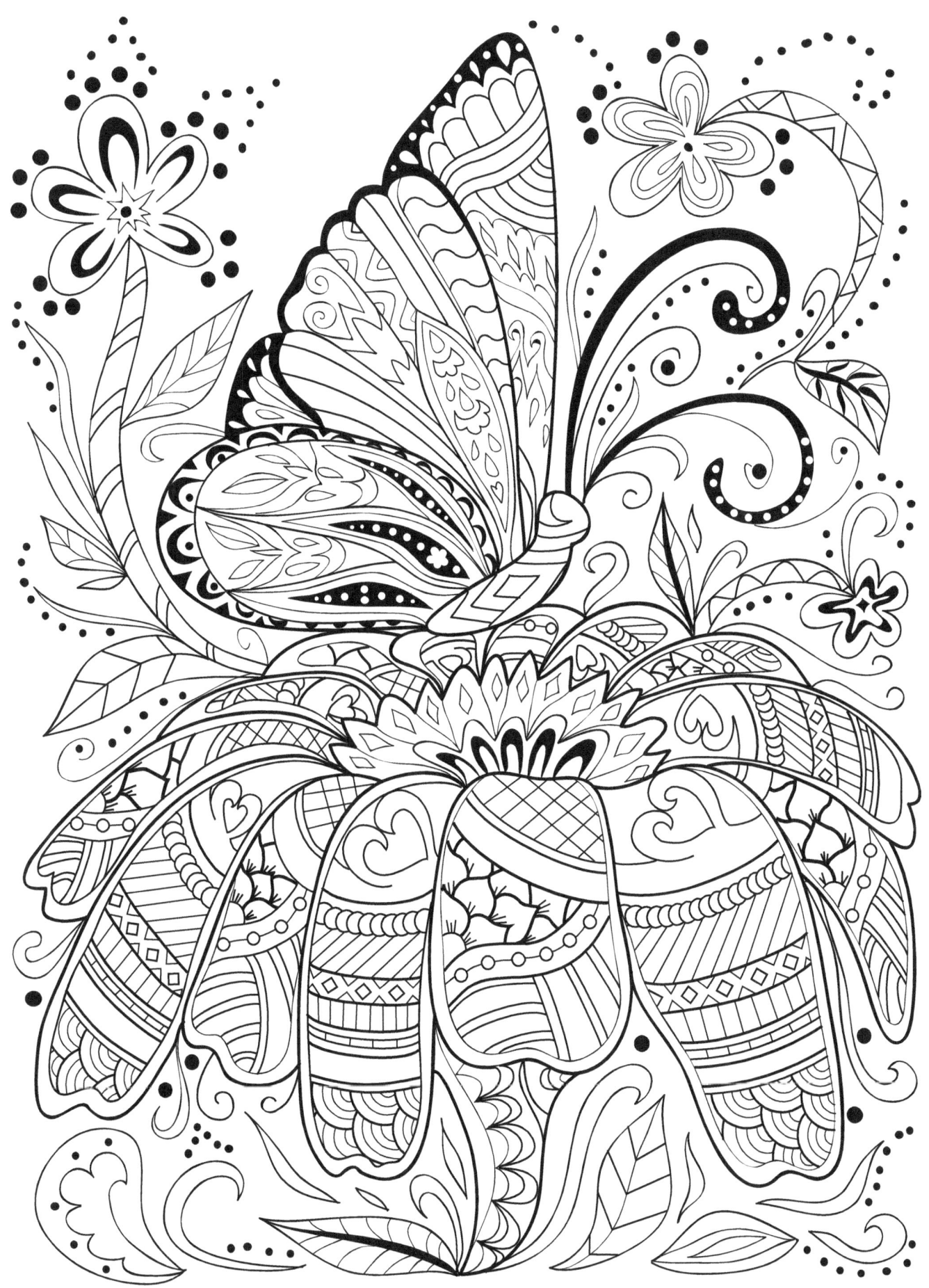

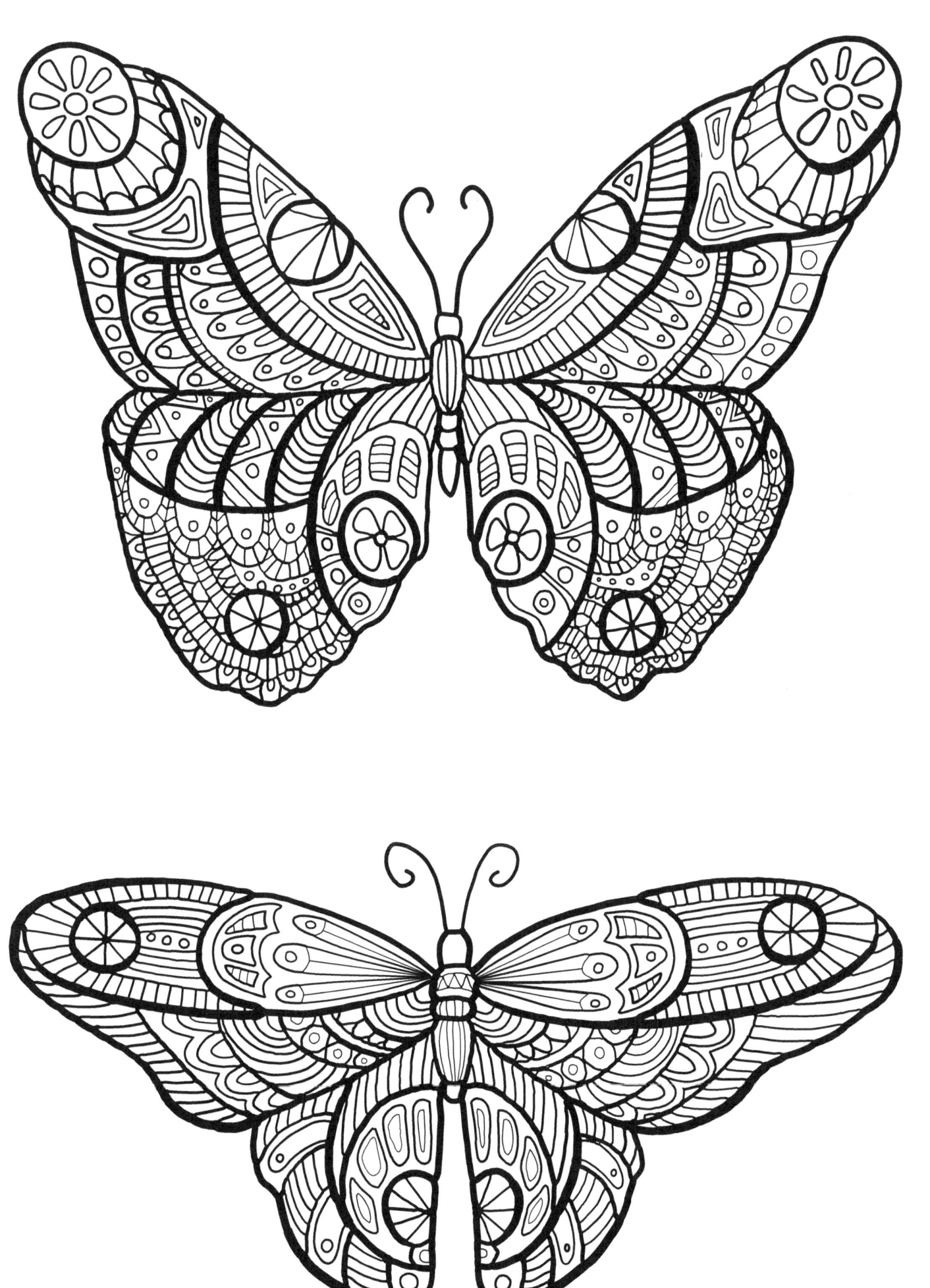

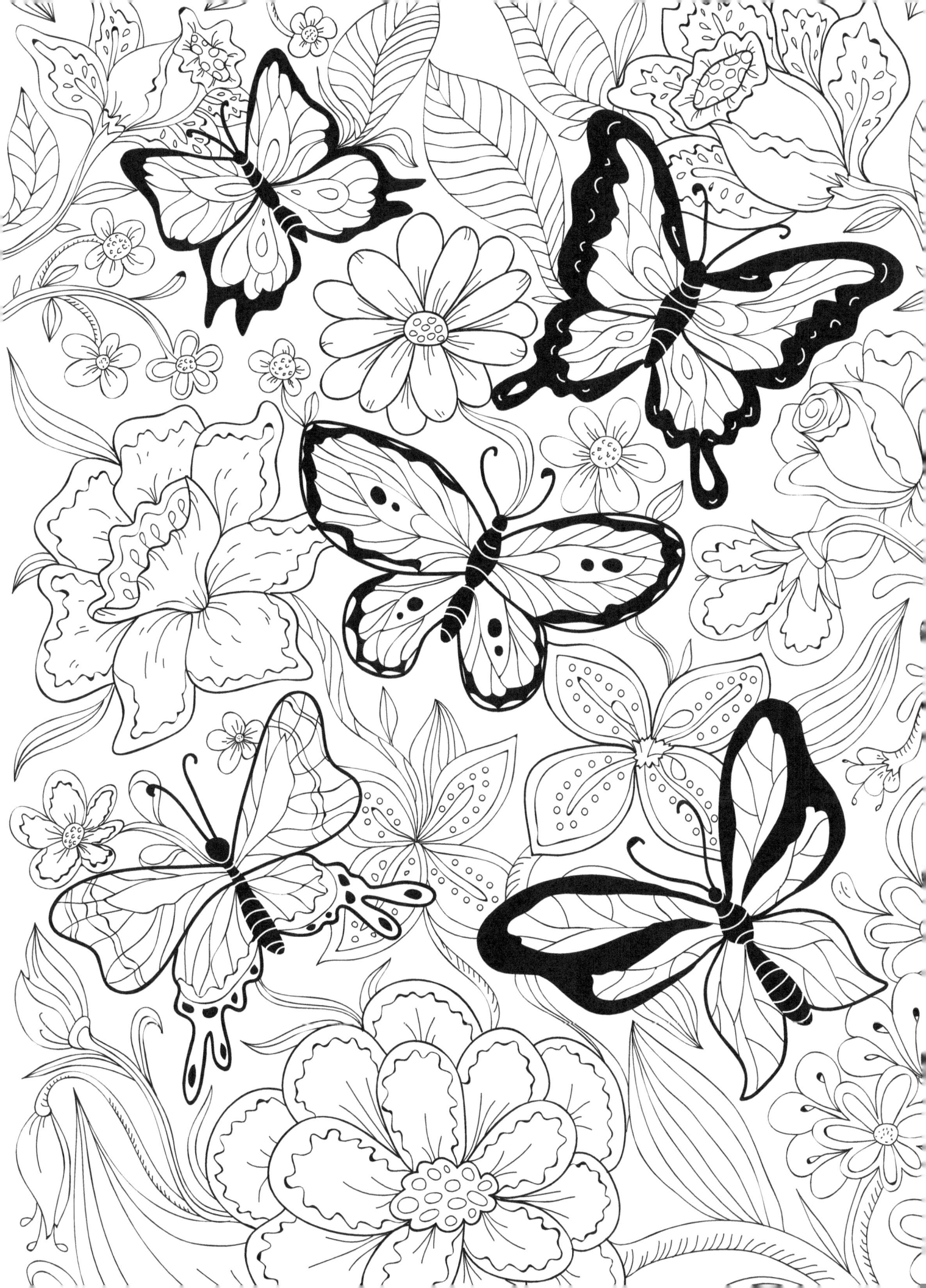

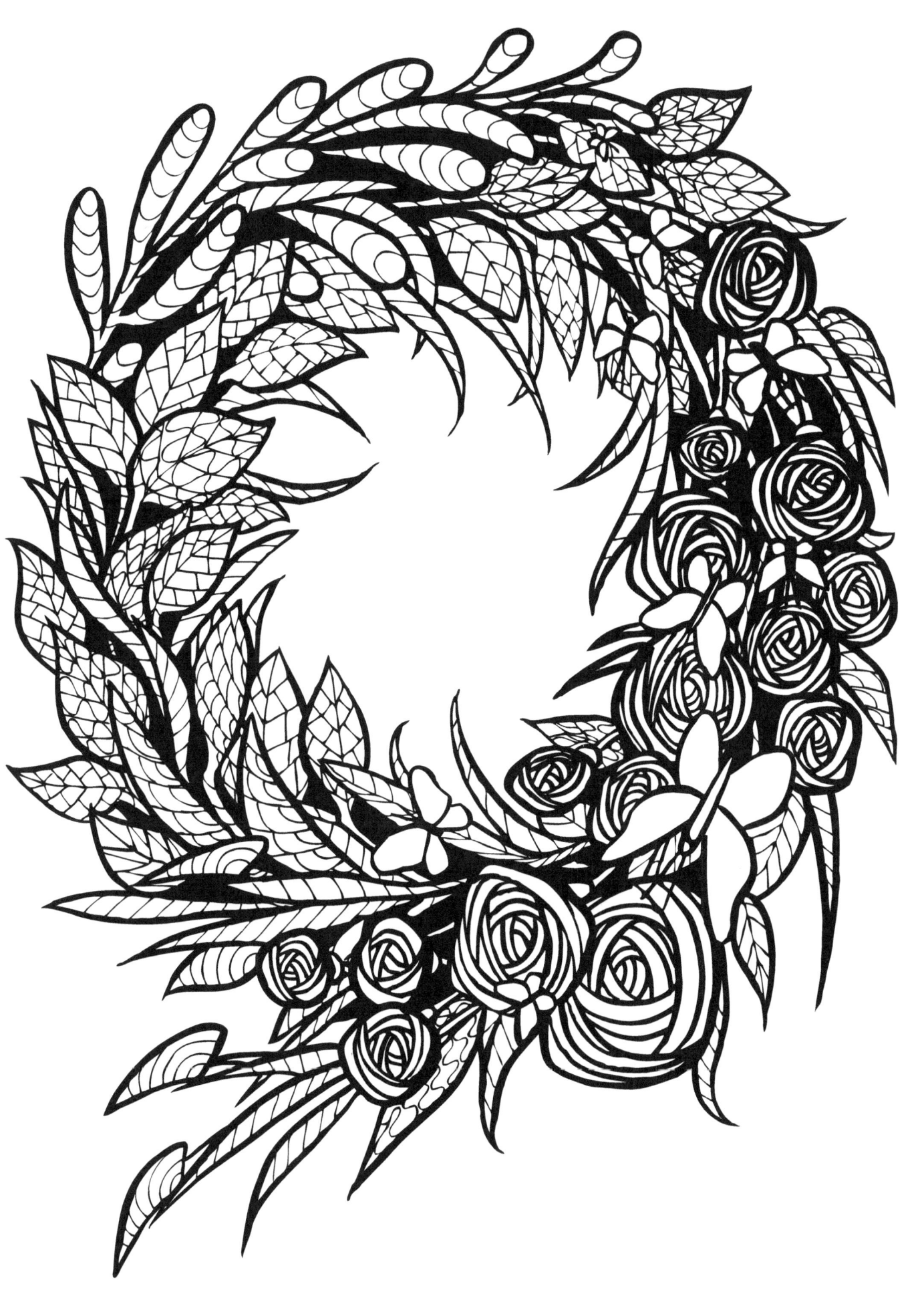

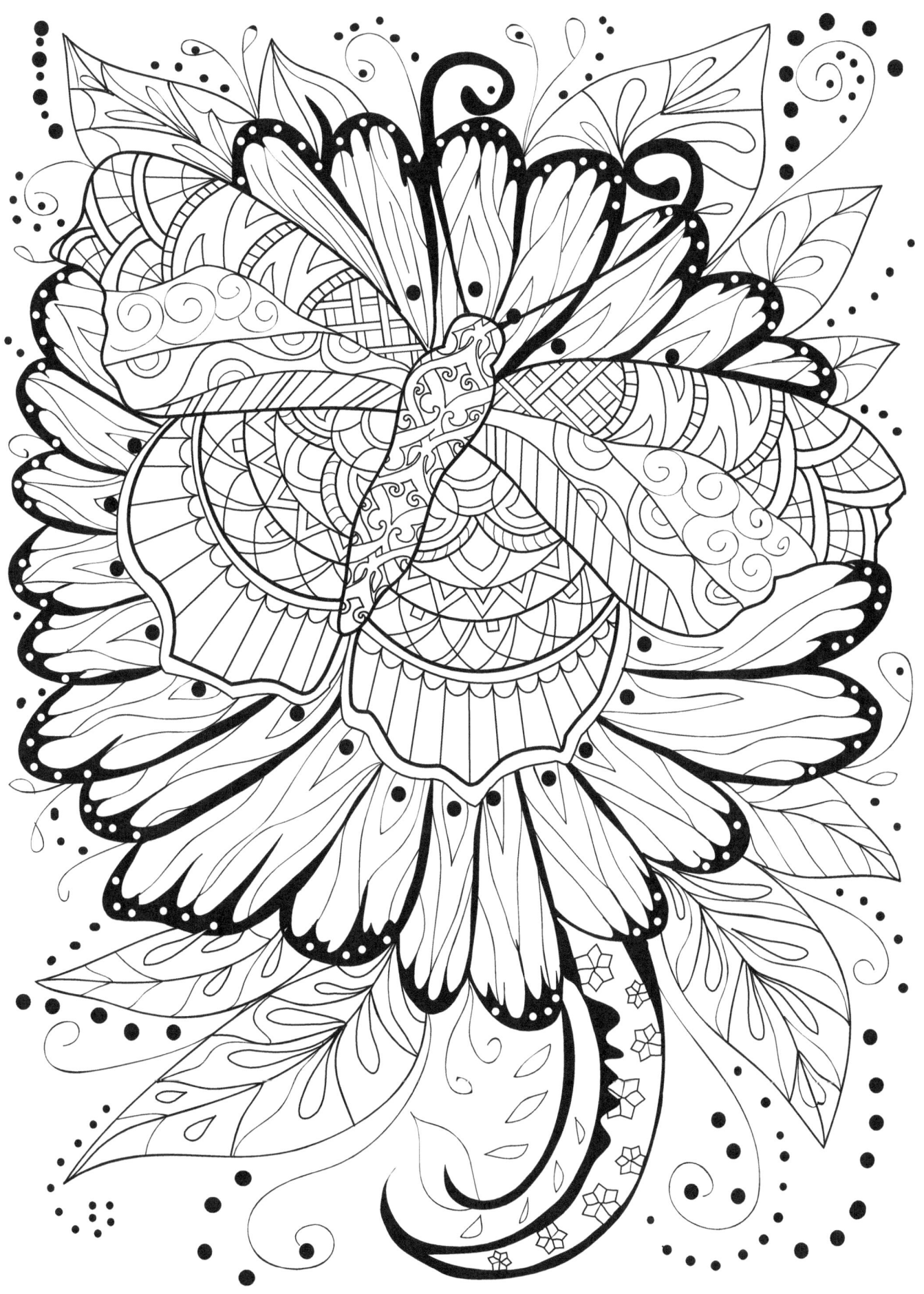

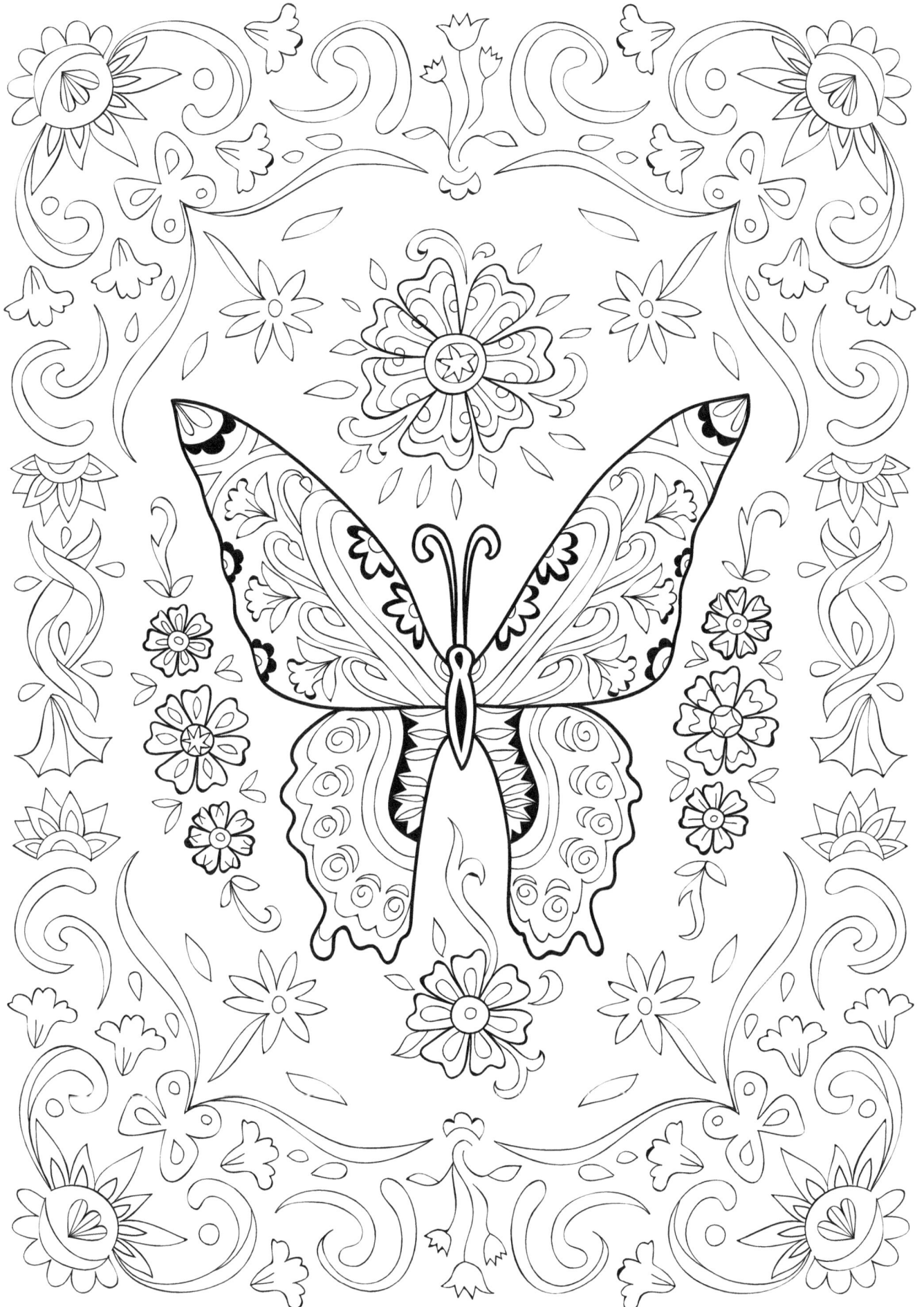

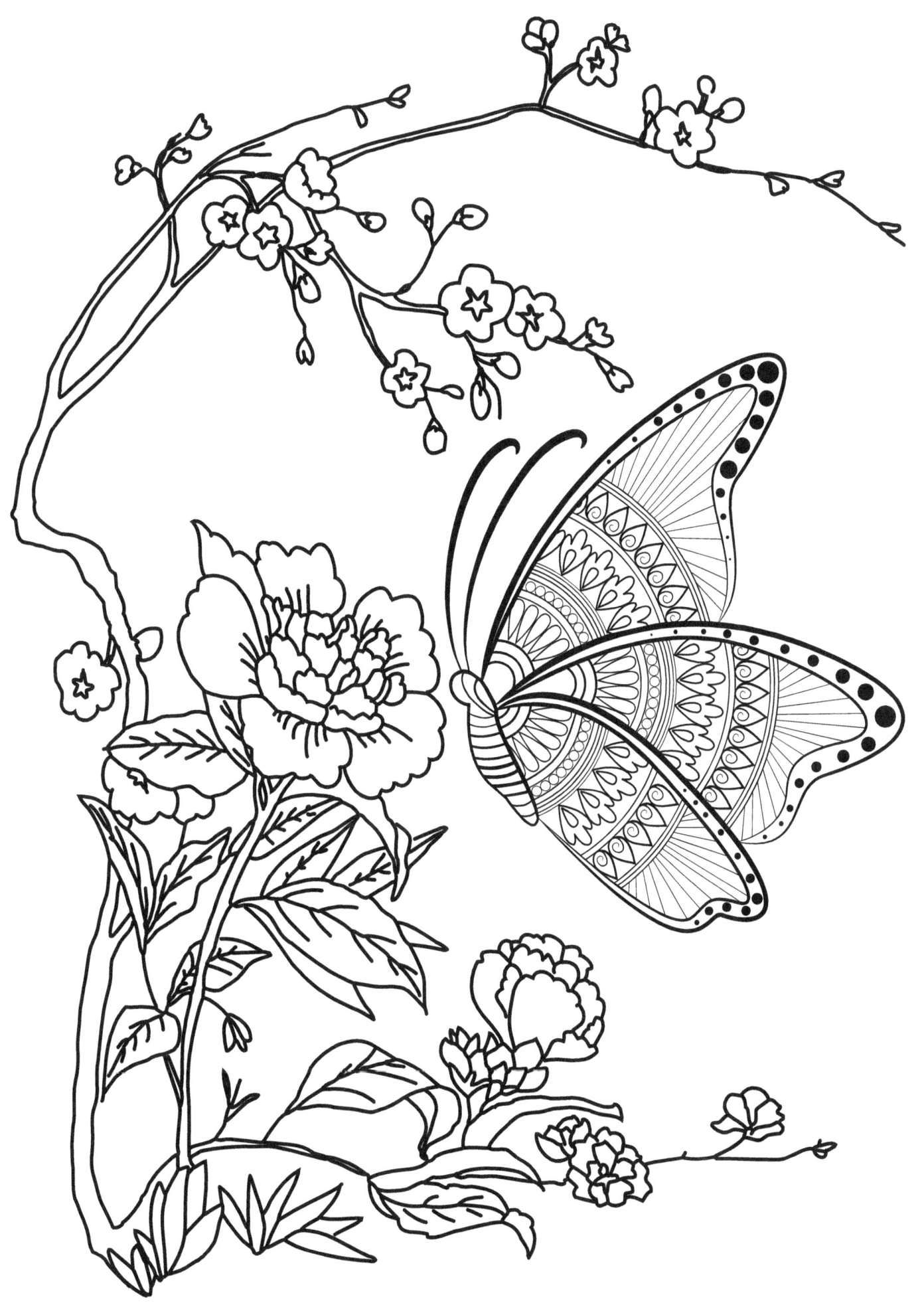

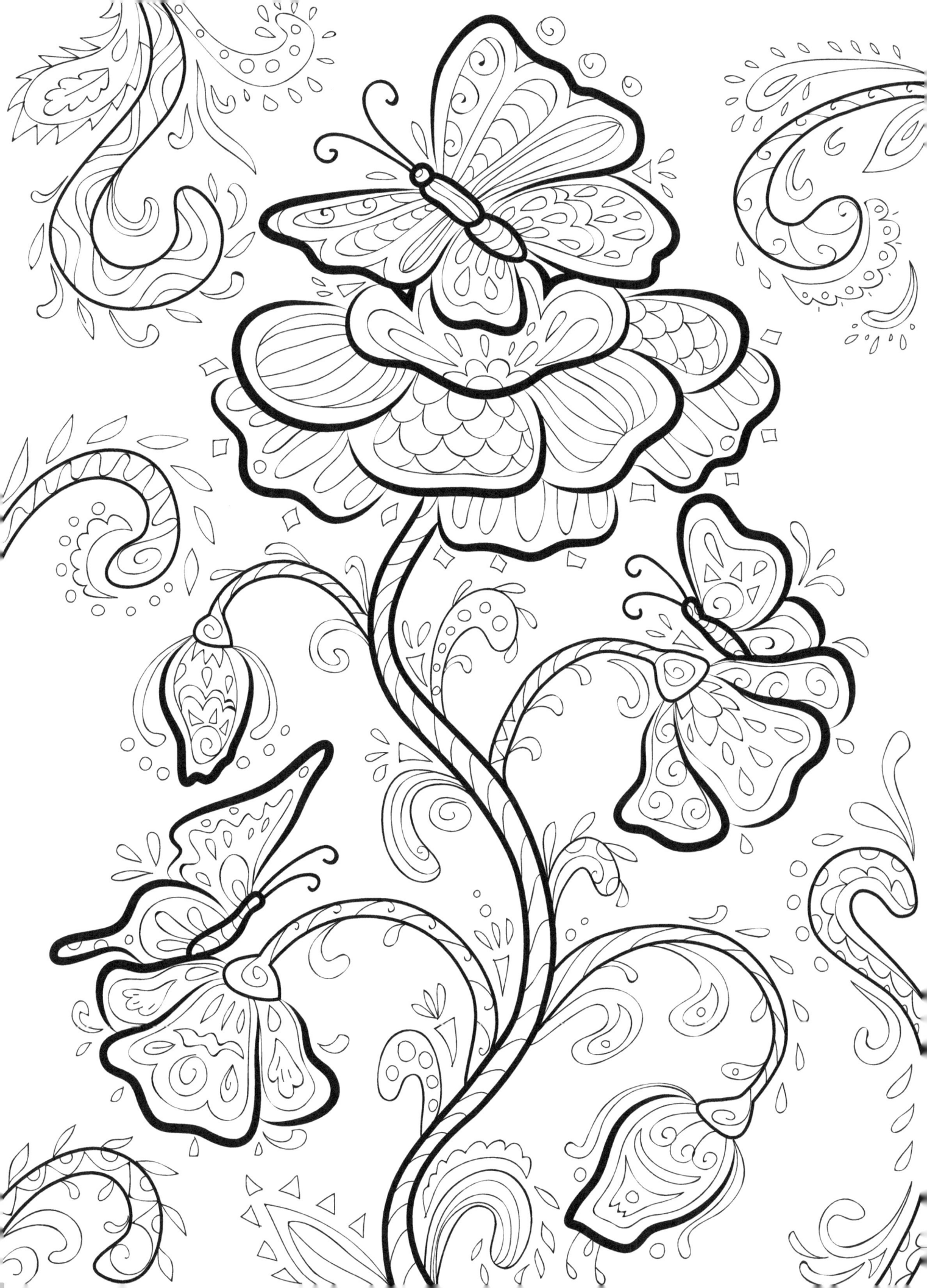

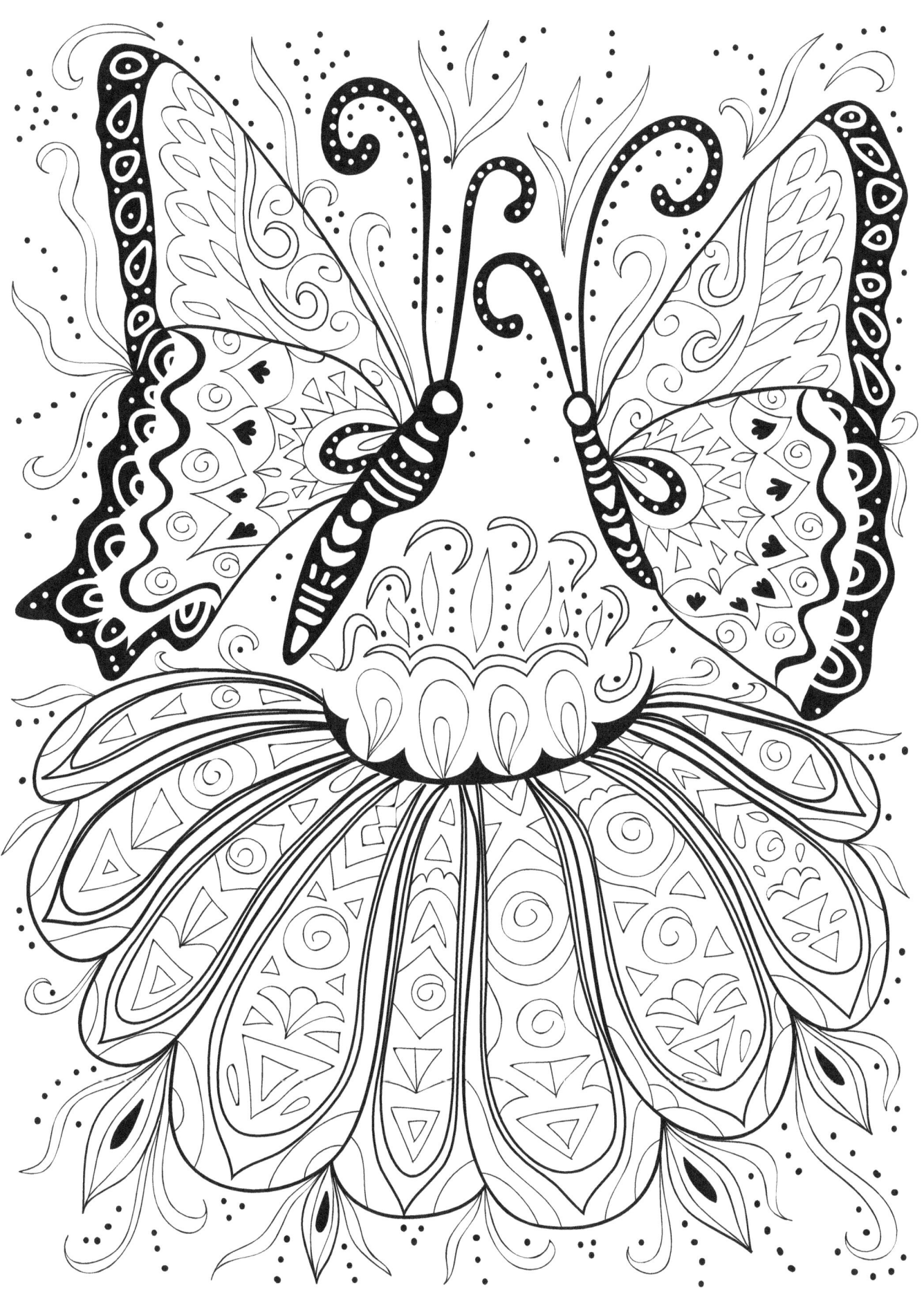

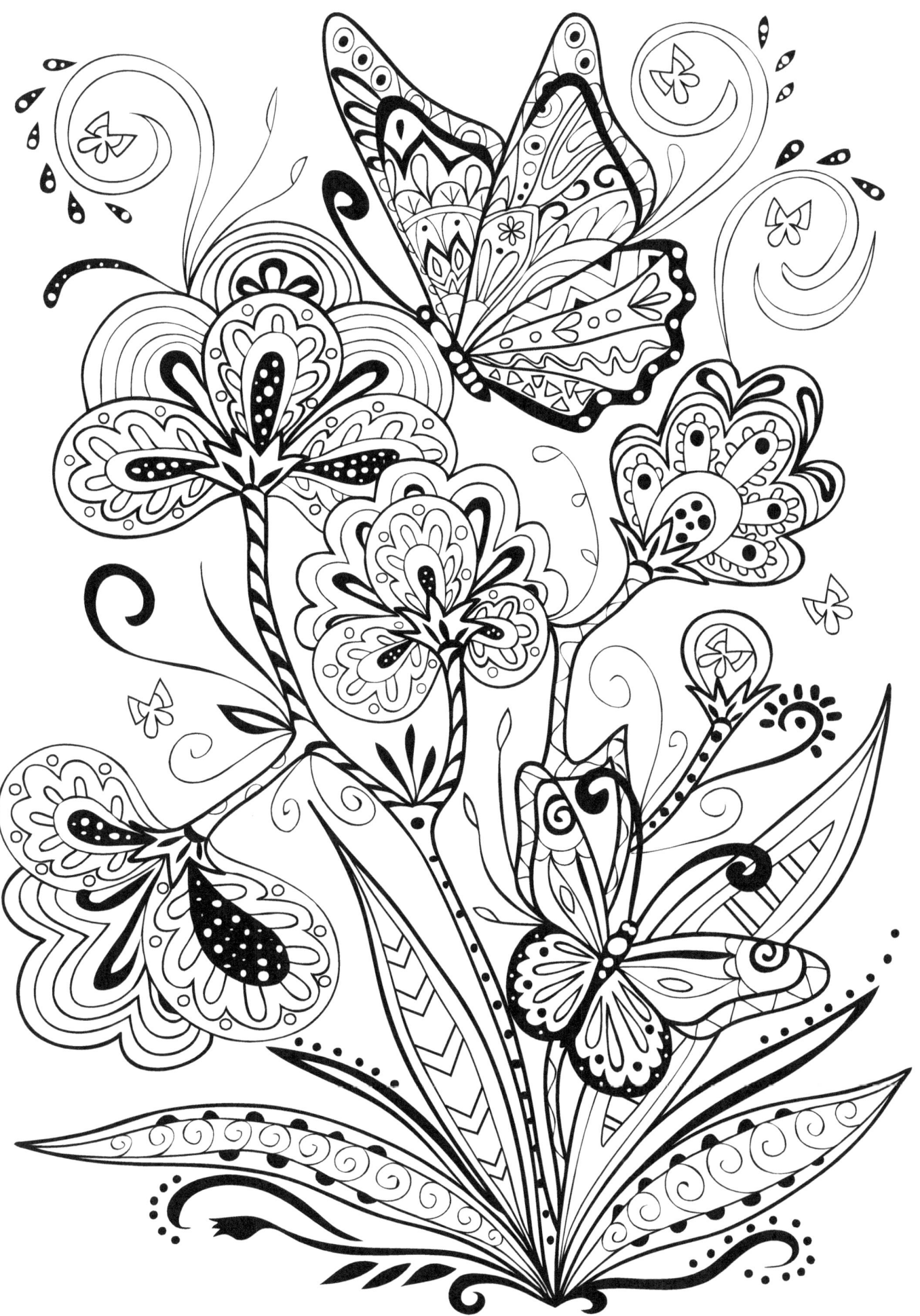

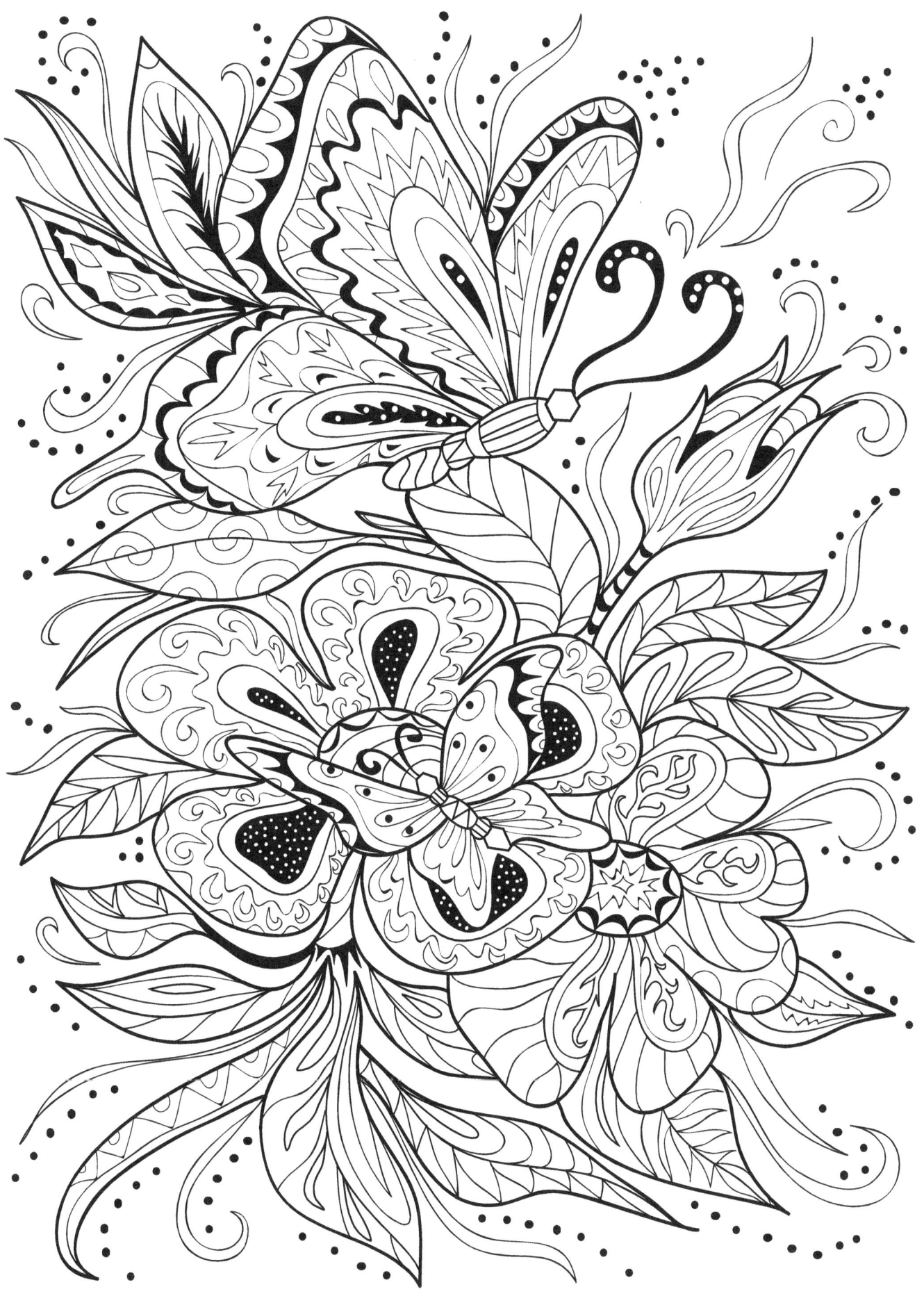

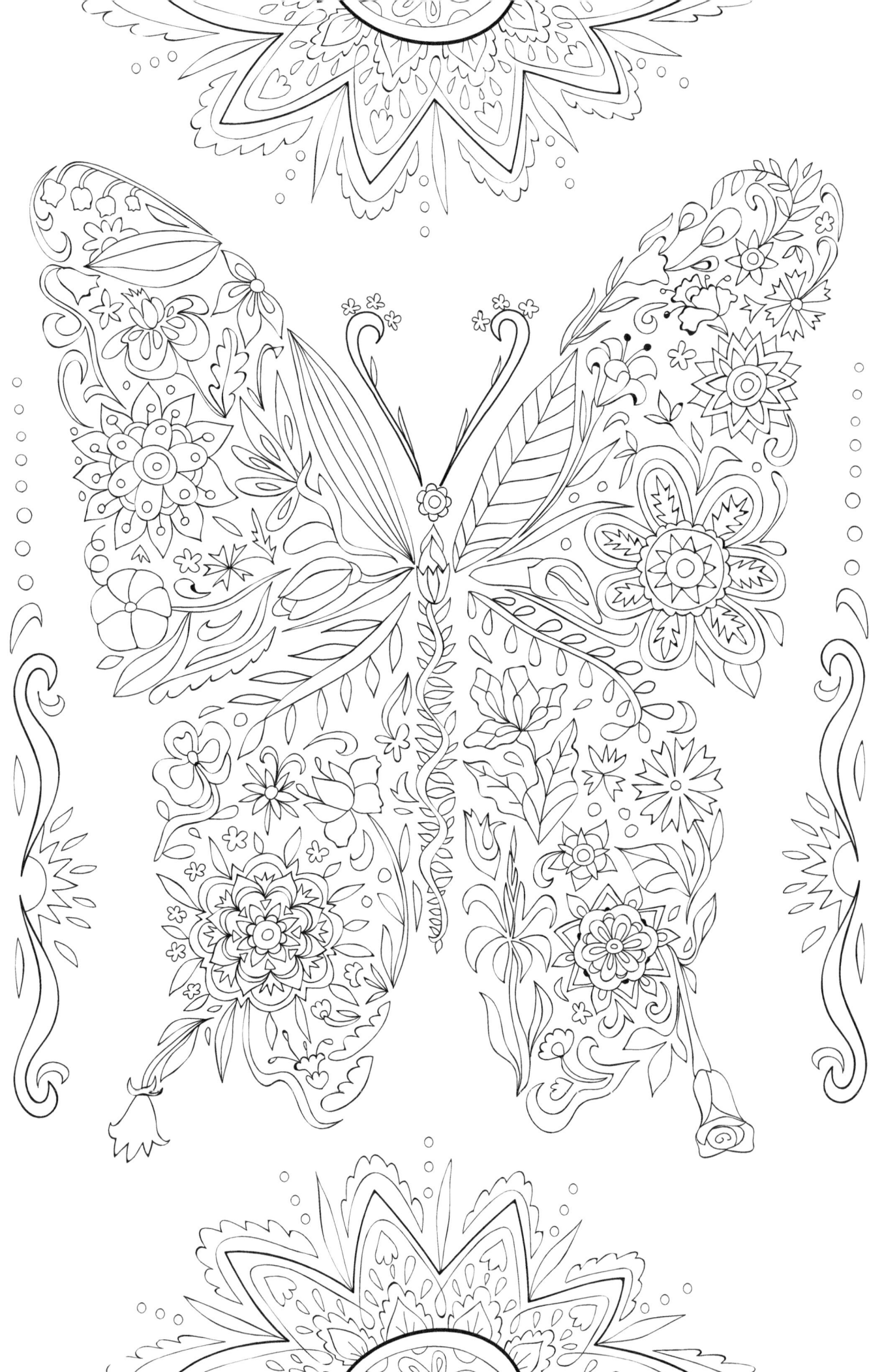

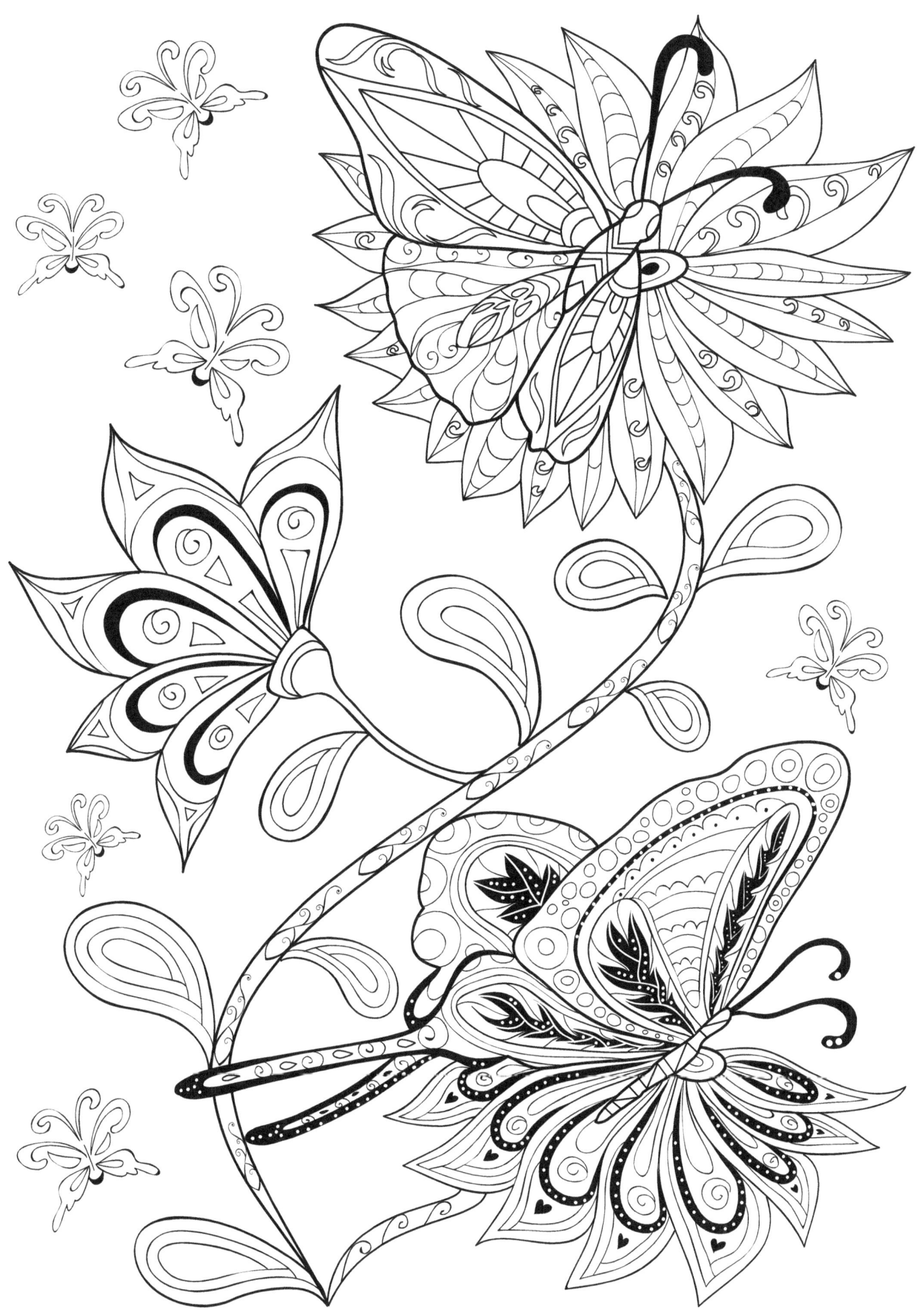

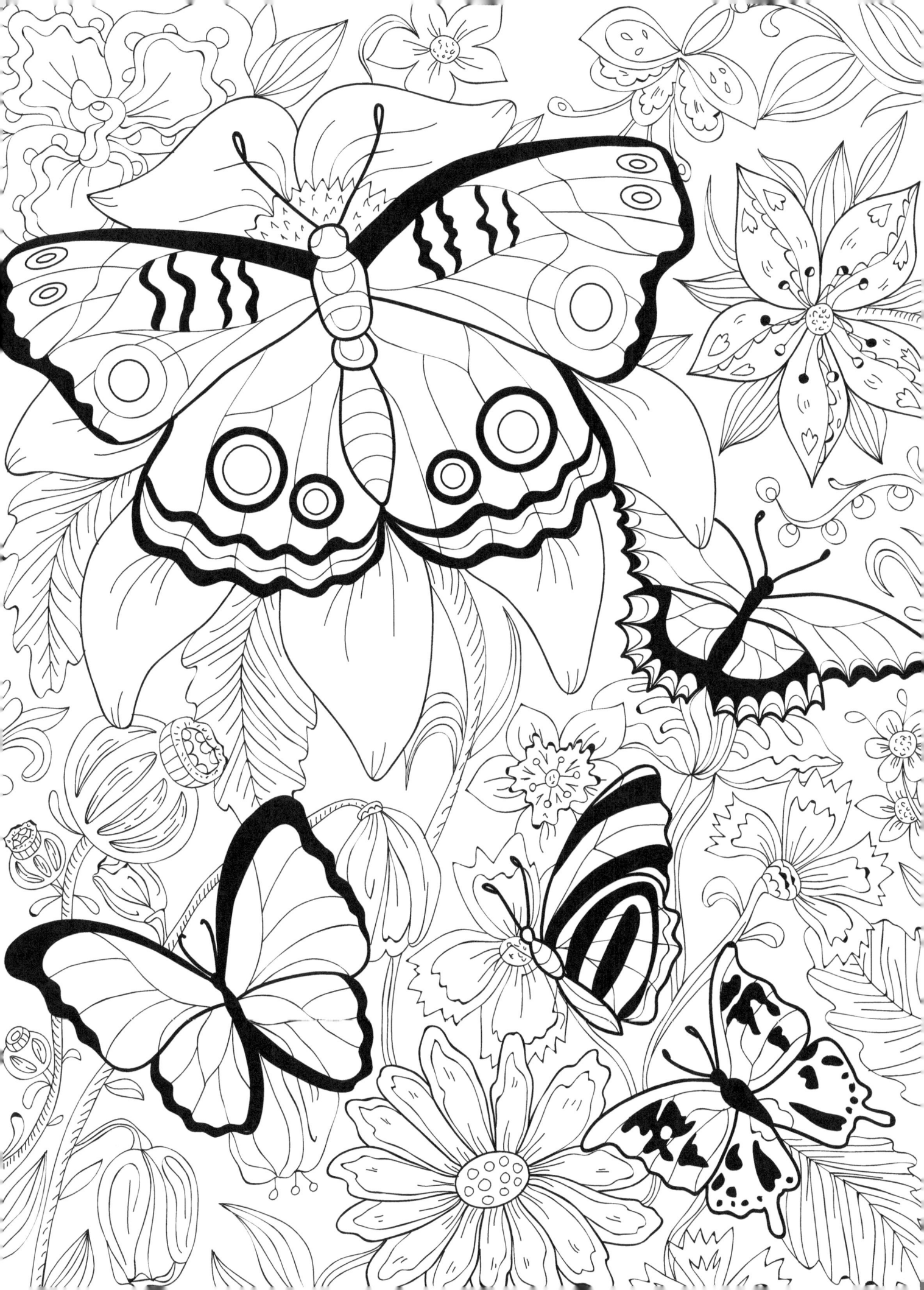

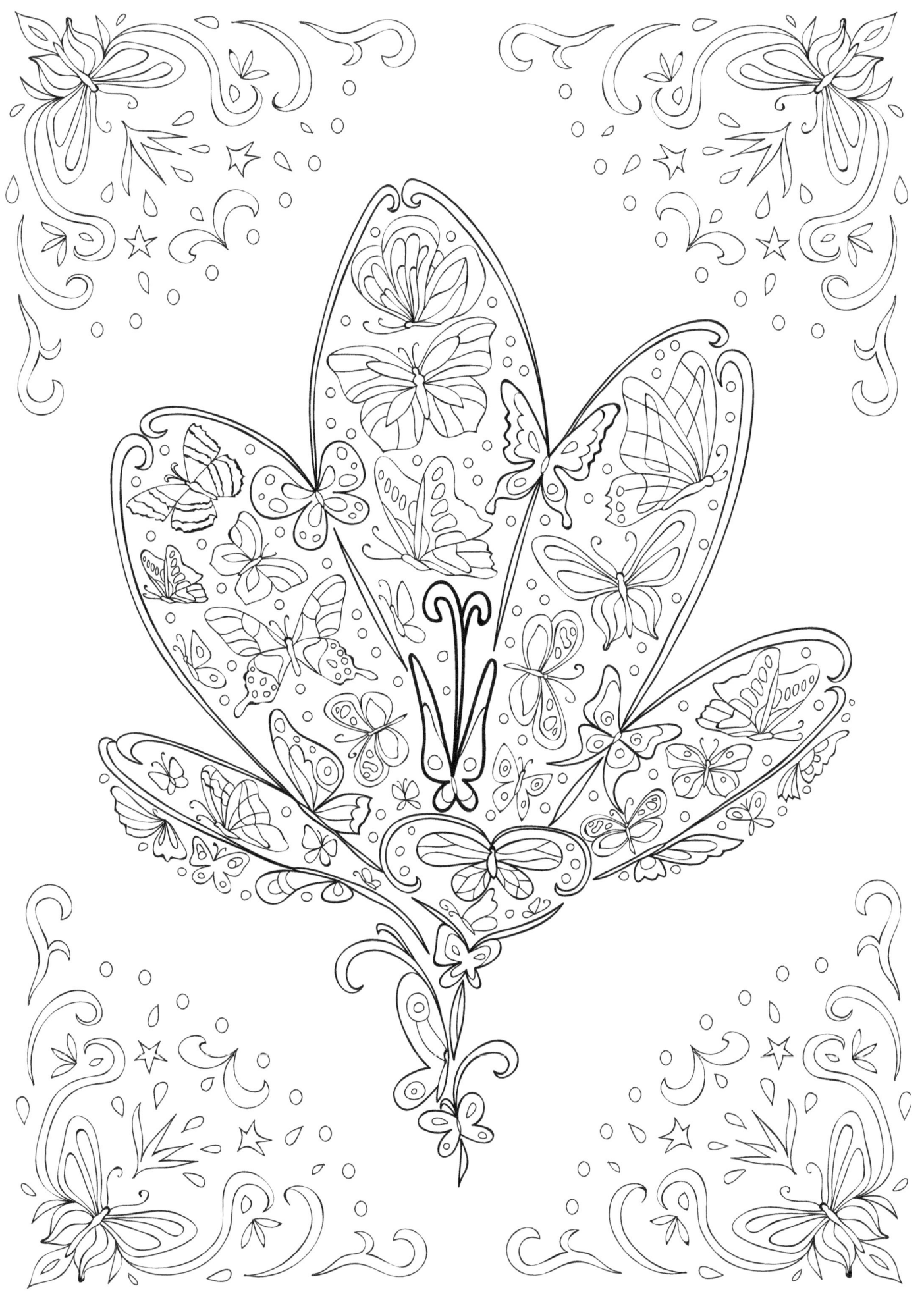

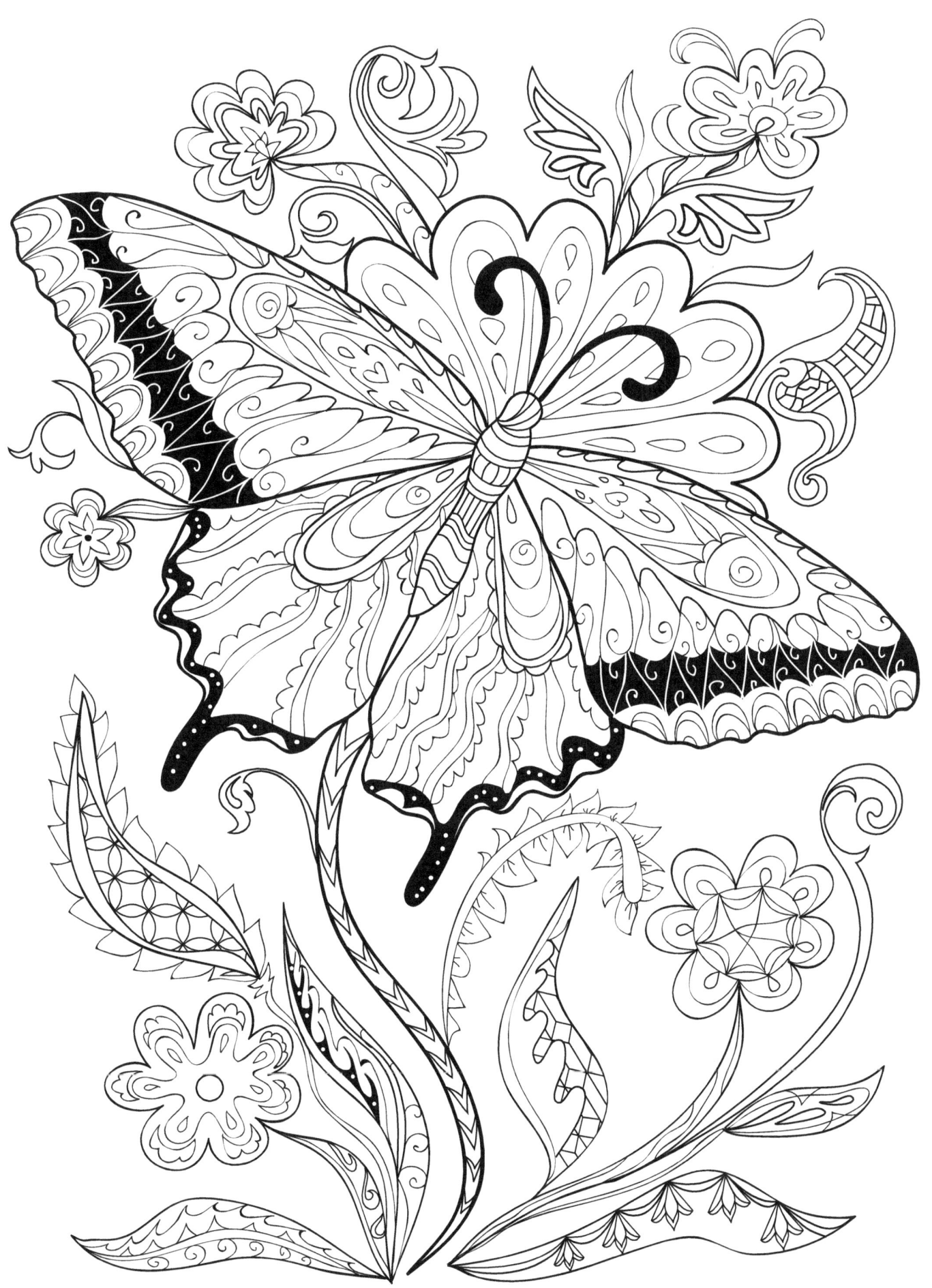

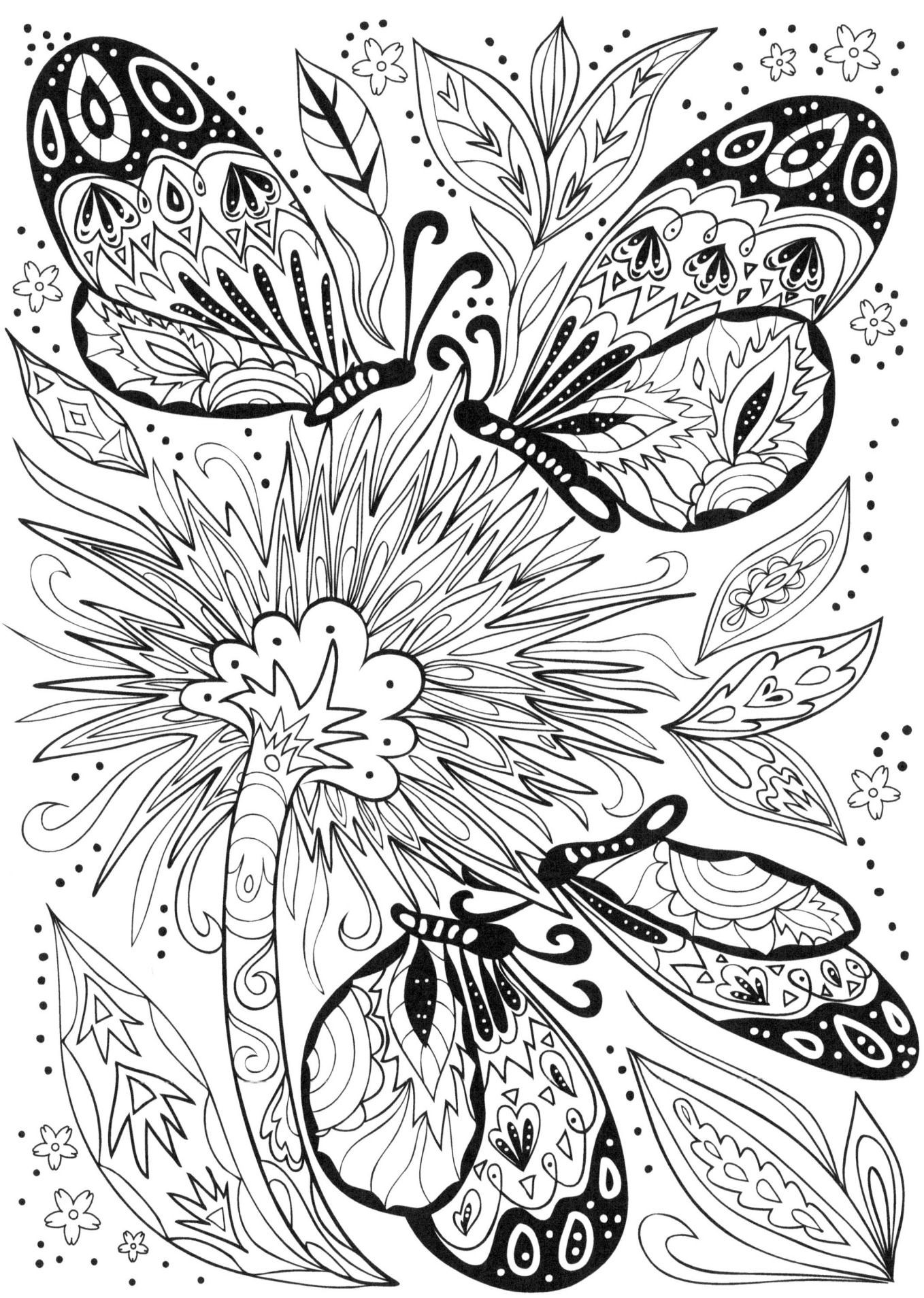

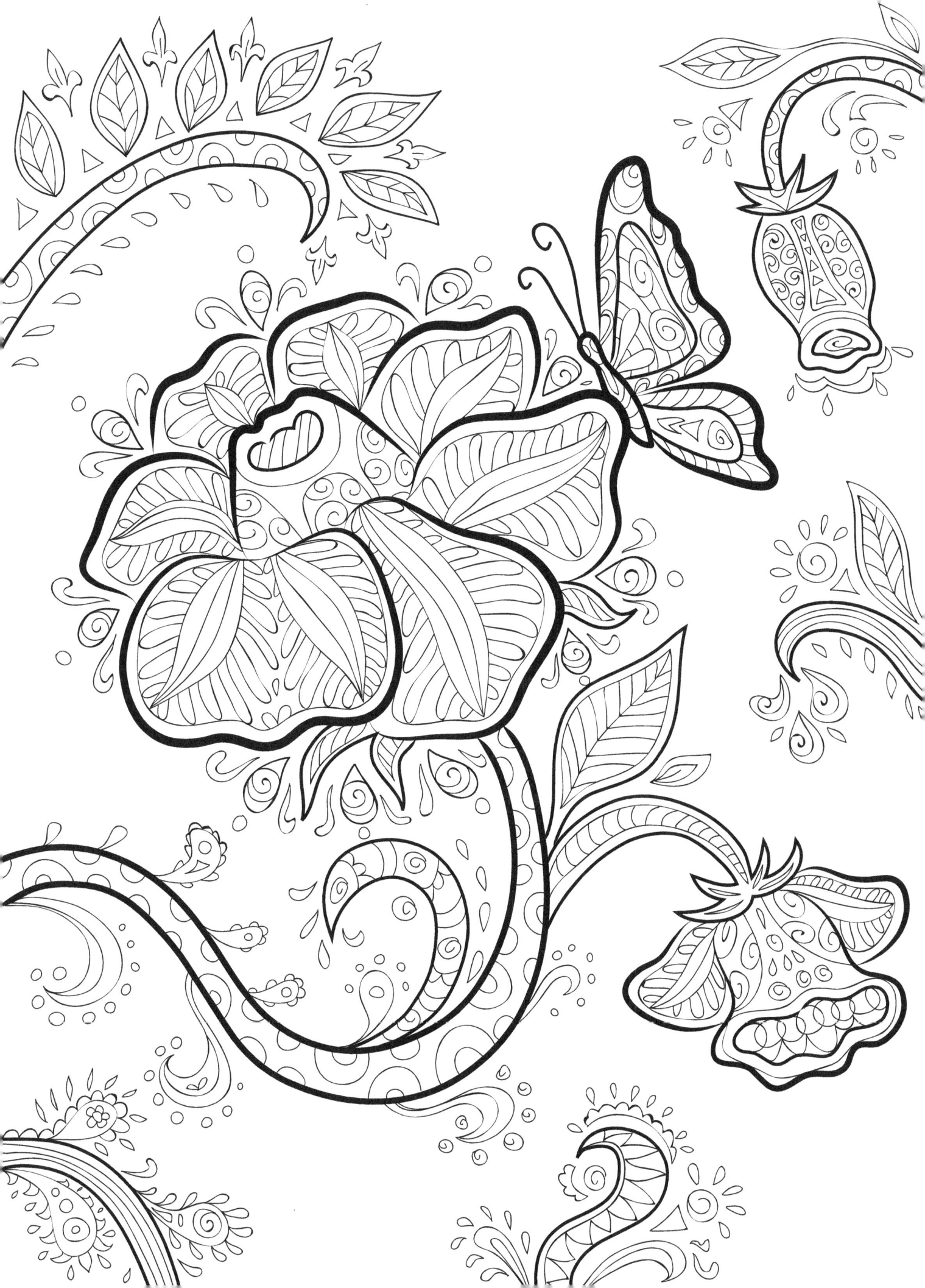

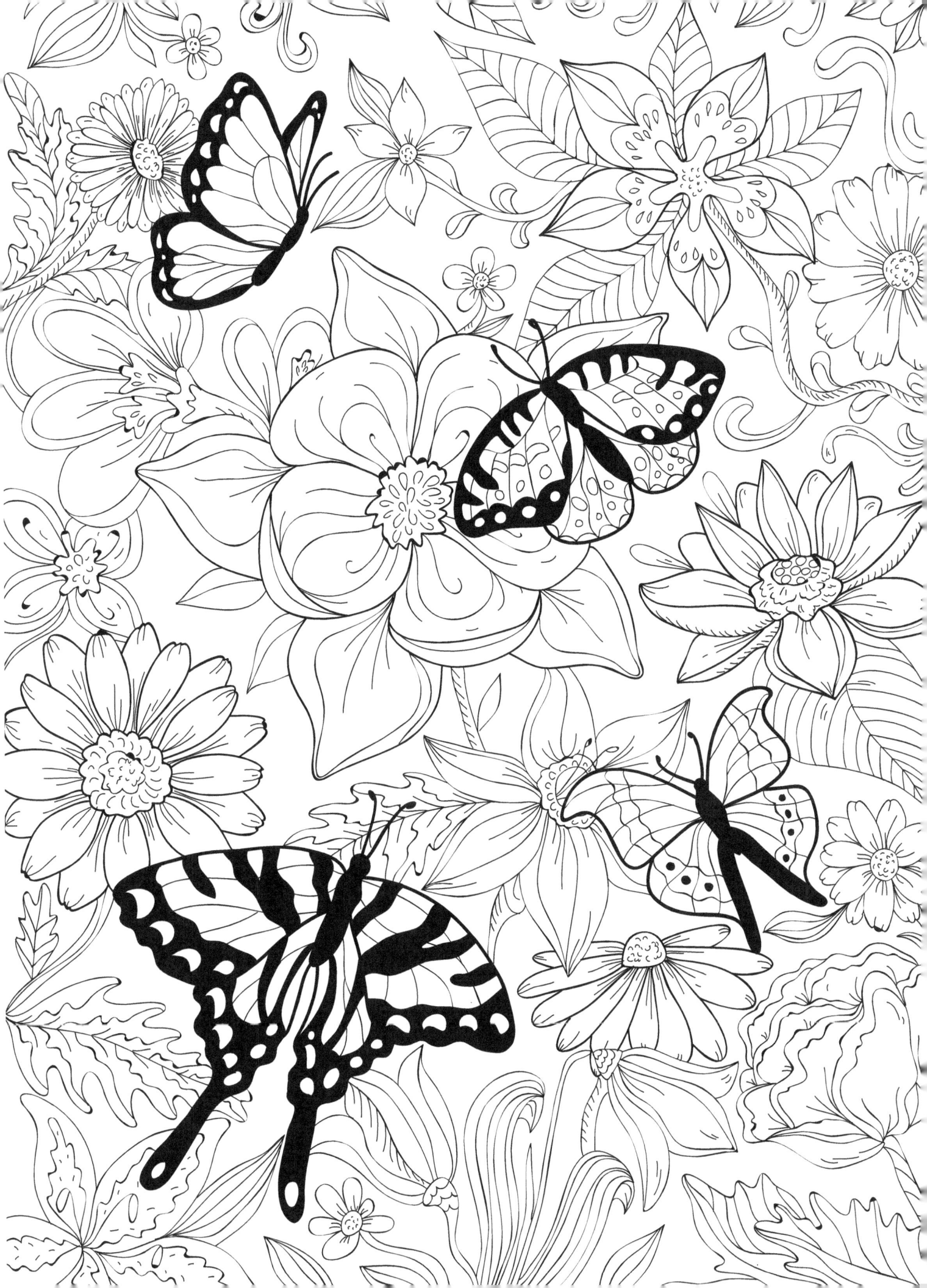

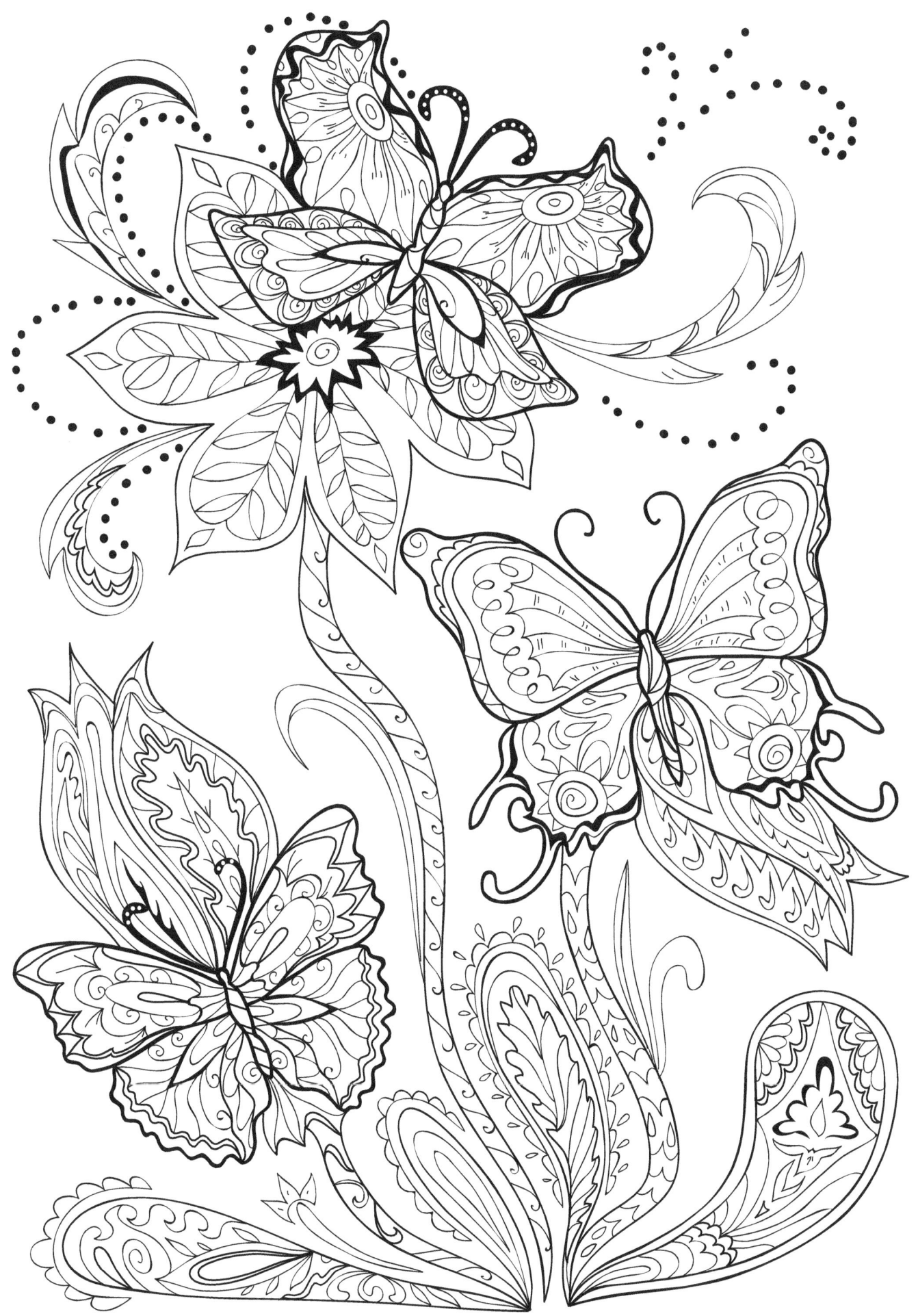

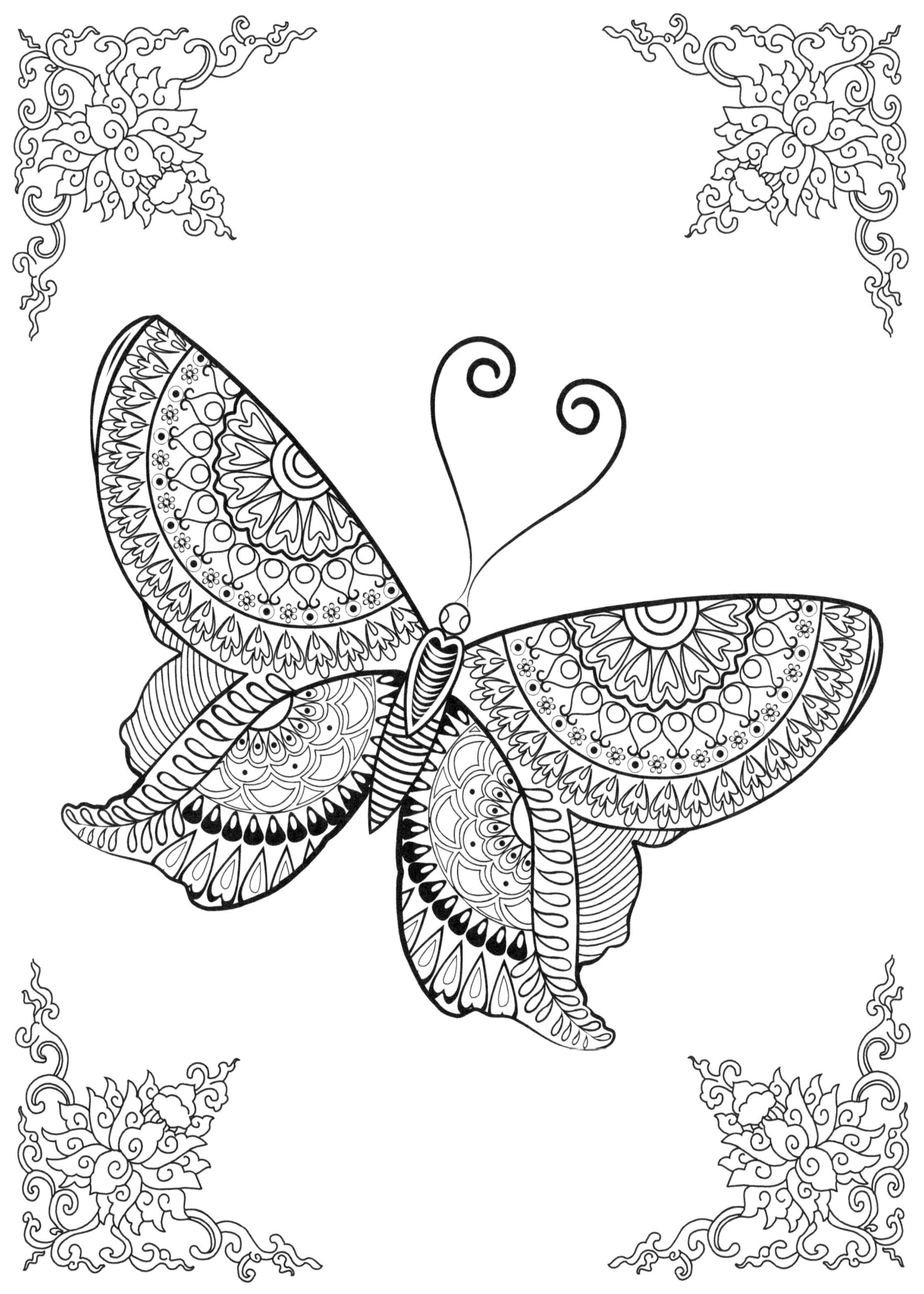

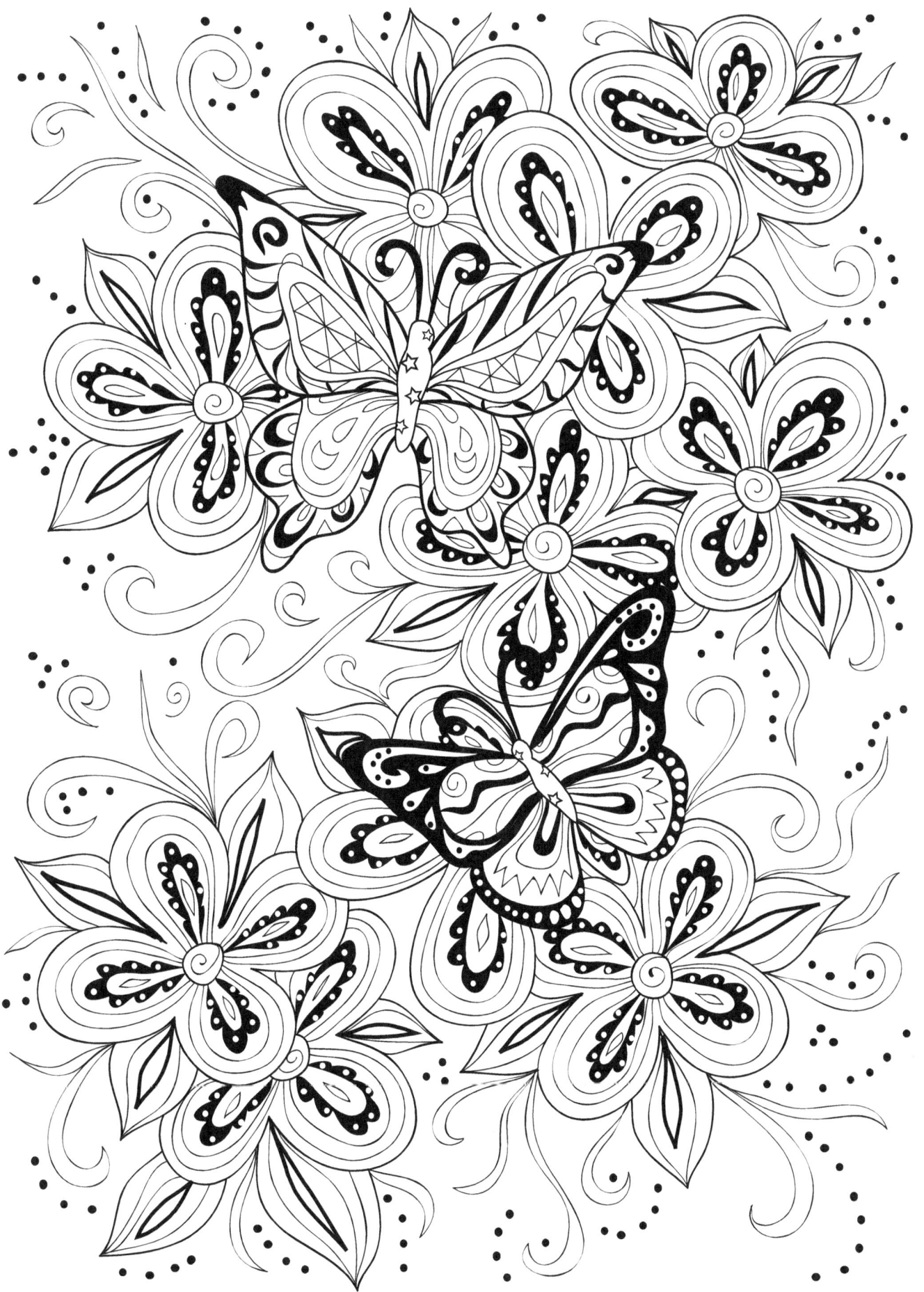

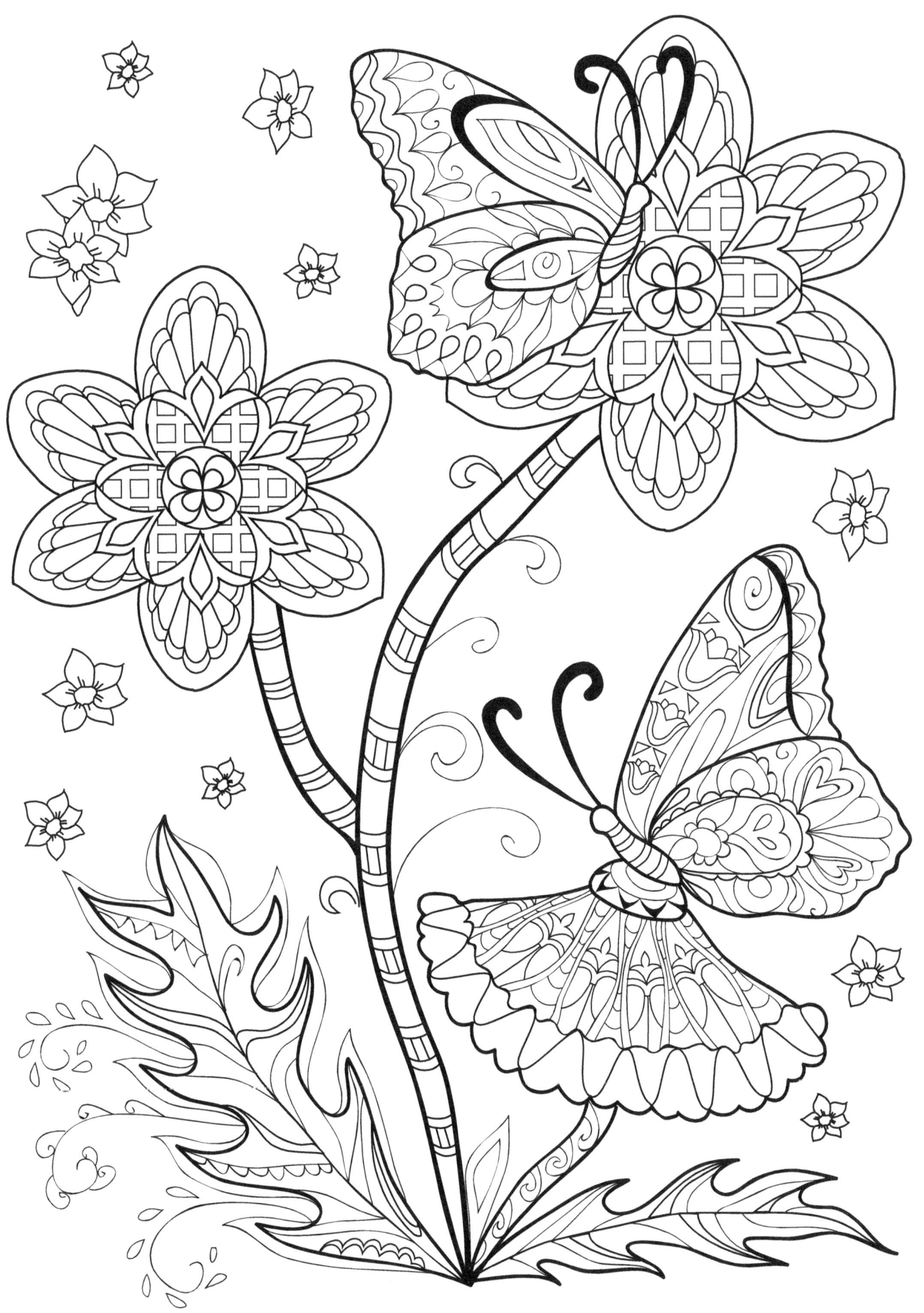

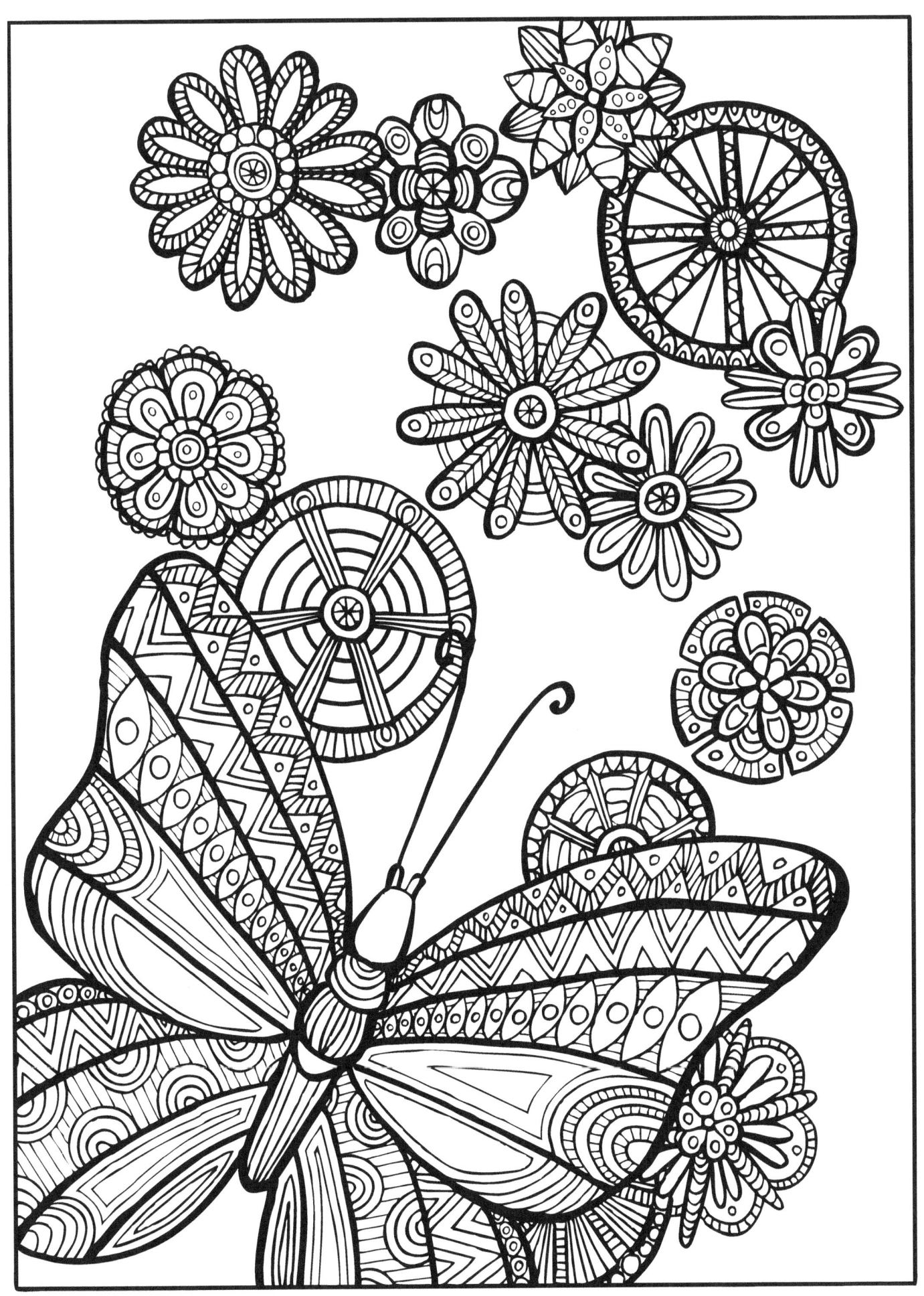

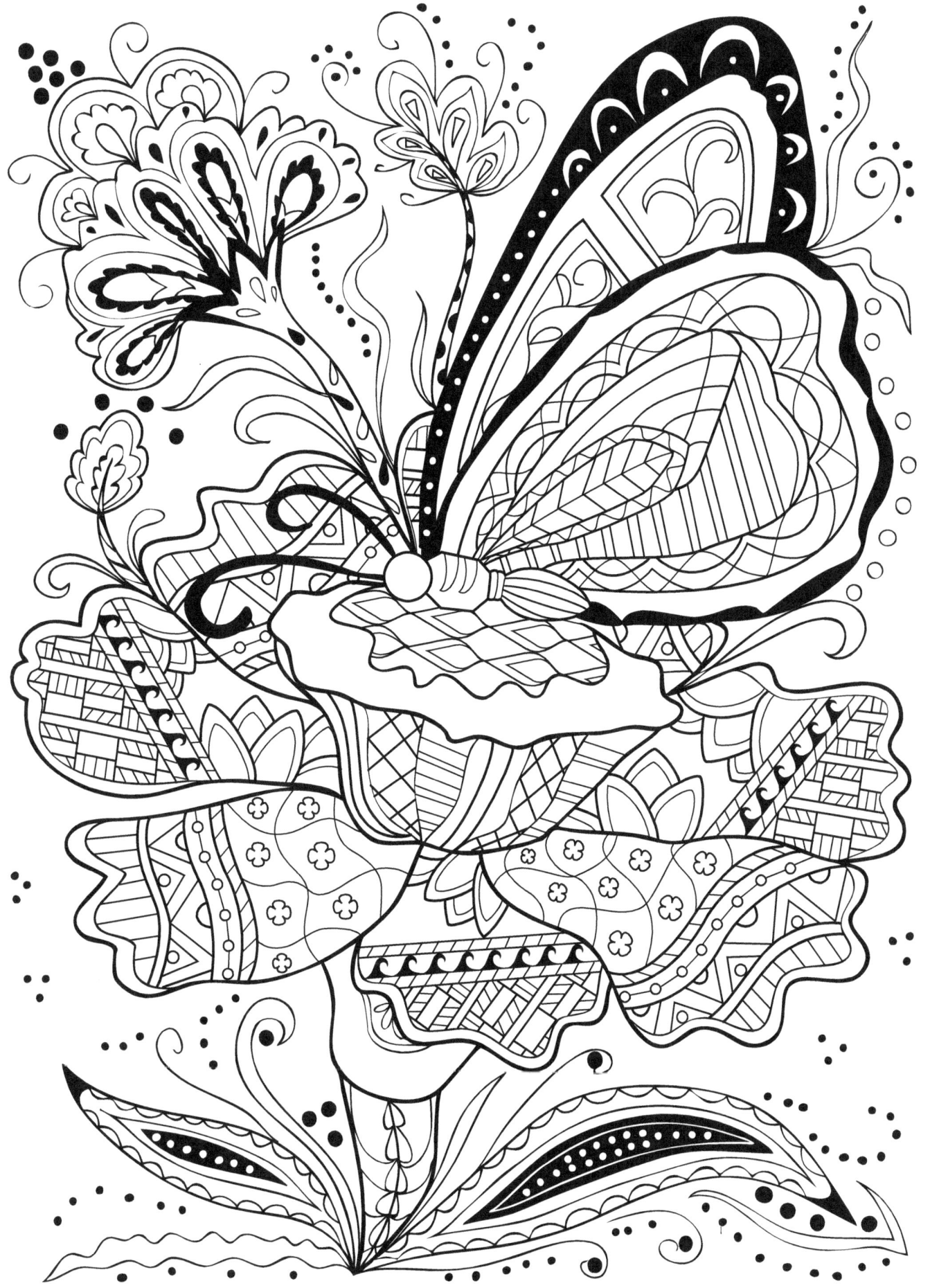

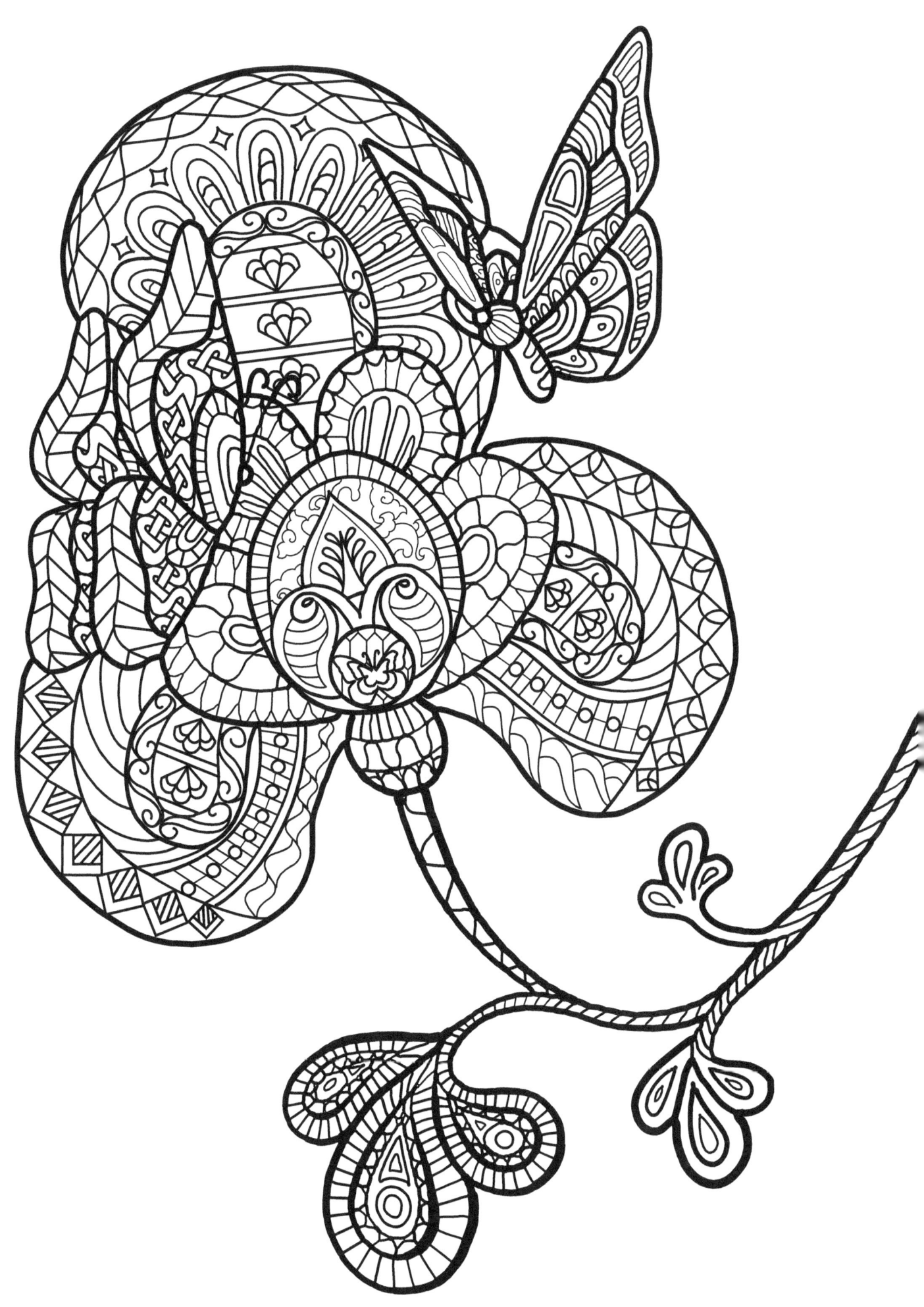

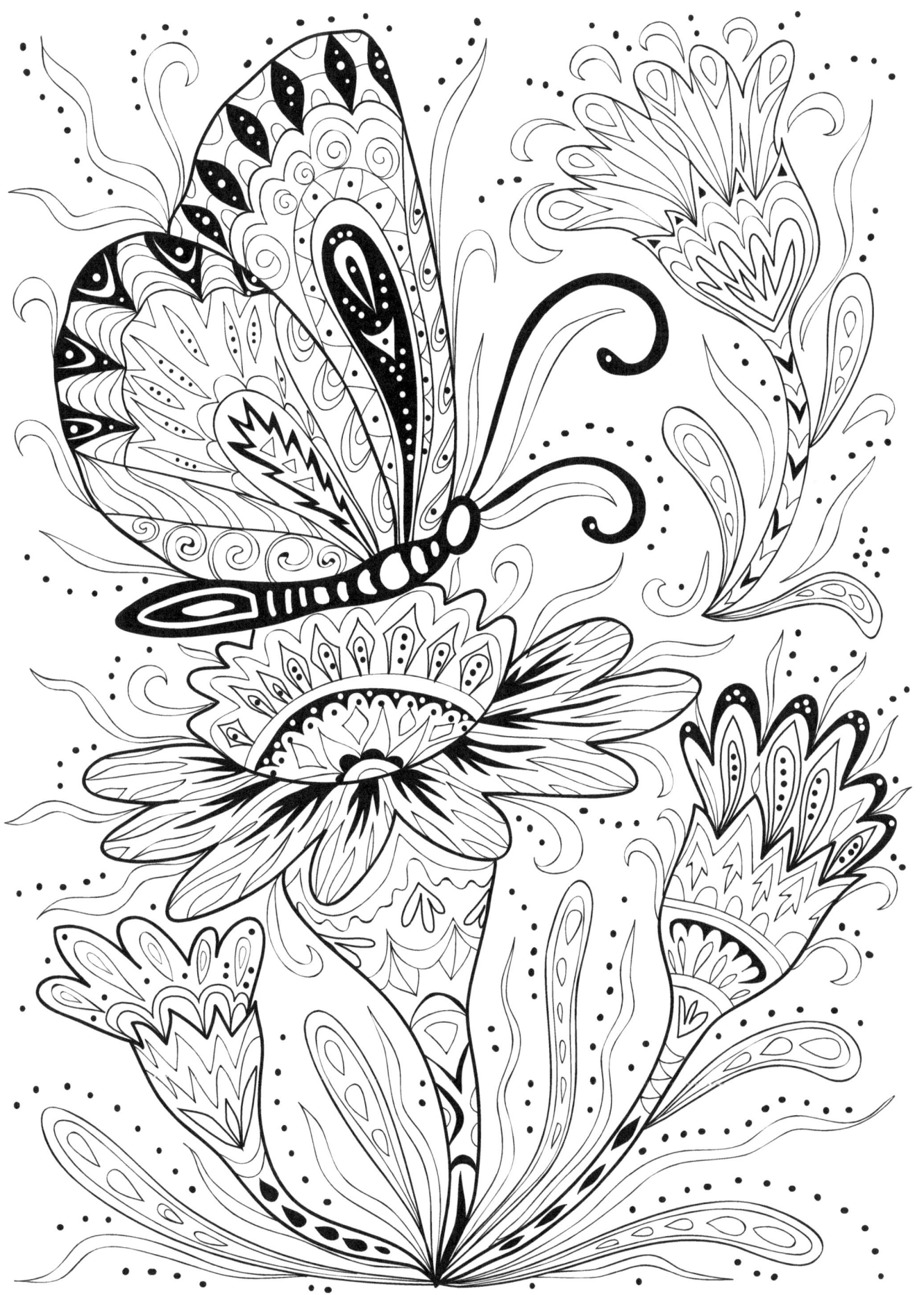

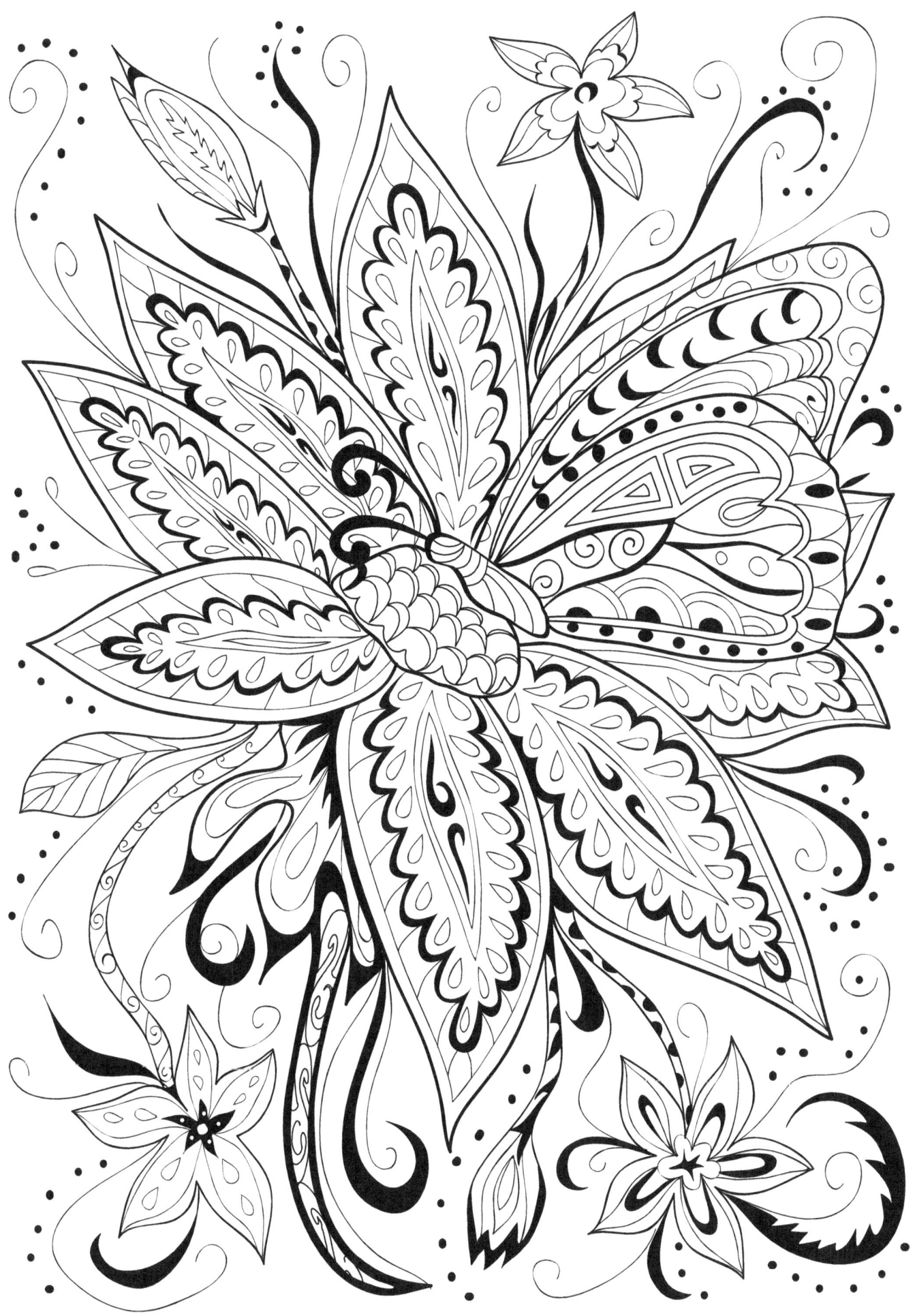

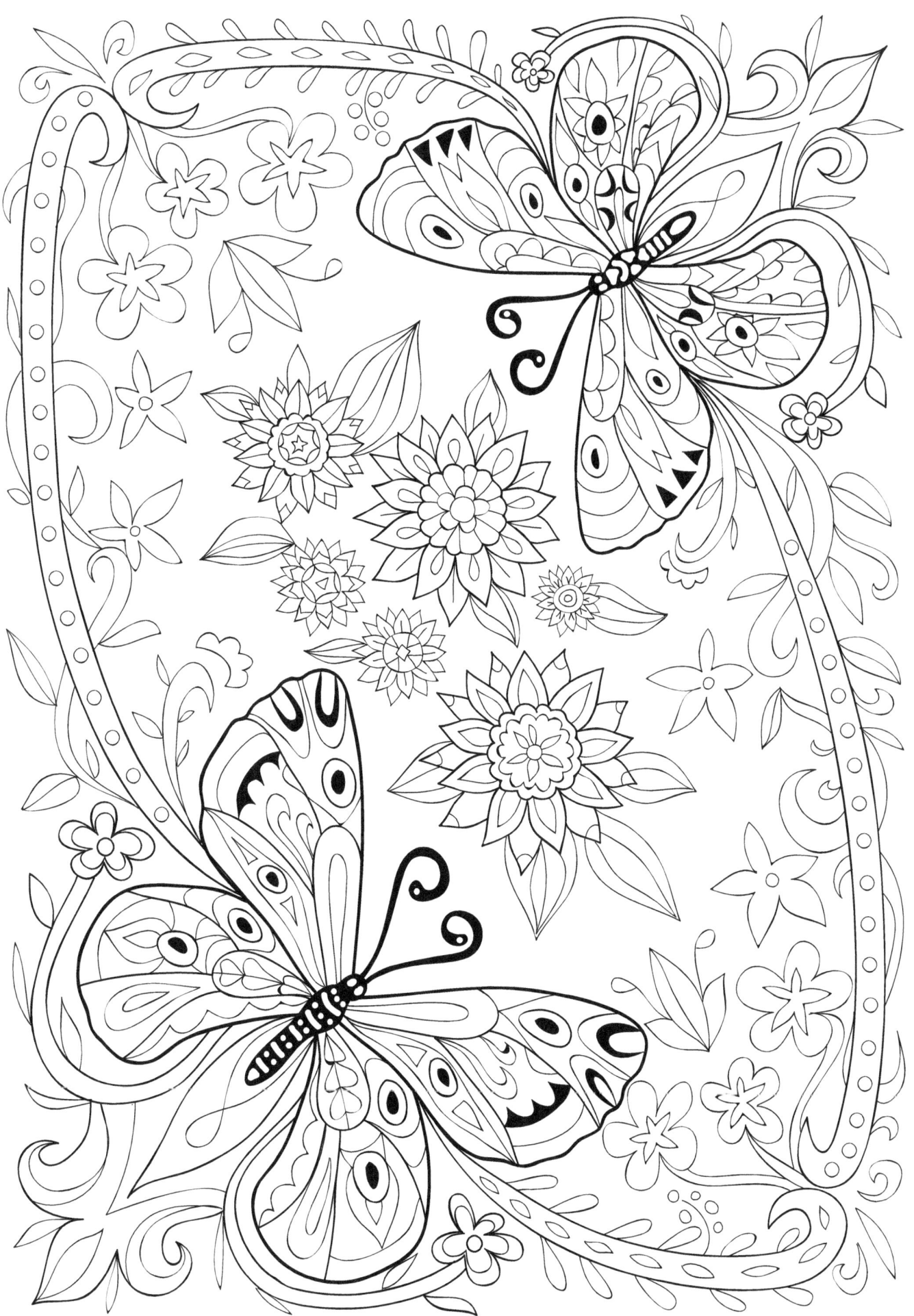